1

Scientific and Esoteric Encyclopedia of UFOs, Aliens and Extraterrestrial Gods

Volume IV: A (An-unperson-Anunnaki)
From a set of 20 volumes.
*** *** ***

Maximillien de Lafayette

Volume IV

SCIENTIFIC AND ESOTERIC ENCYCLOPEDIA OF UFOS, ALIENS AND EXTRATERRESTRIAL GODS

The world's first and most authoritative encyclopedia of its kind!!

Published in the United States of America and Germany.

Printed by Times Square Press. New York.
Date of Publication: July 22, 2014.

Scientific and Esoteric Encyclopedia of UFOs, Aliens and Extraterrestrial Gods

Volume IV: A (An-unperson-Anunnaki) from a set of 20 volumes.

Maximillien de Lafayette

*** *** ***

Times Square Press
New York Berlin Paris Madrid
2014

Table Of Contents

- Hitler-American scientists meeting after WWII.
- Flying discs, triangular anti-gravity aircrafts, tube-shaped crafts, and a huge mothership.
- The Russians out of the loop!
- Talking to Hitler.
- Working with Nazi scientists and Hitler's engineers.
- Anti-gravitational triangular craft.
- Anti-gravity Levity Disc of John Searl.
- Antu.
- Anu "Anum".
- Anunna.
- Anunnaki.

*** *** ***

A

Continued from Volume III.

An-unperson: A term coined by George Orwell in 1984, and used to refer to a person whose credentials, diplomas, certificates, and academic degrees were erased from all public records, by a government's agency, in order to discredit him or her, and/or to destroy his/her credibility. Usually, an-unperson, is a qualified, well-informed, or an experienced individual who has previously worked on government's secret projects, or black operations, and later became a whistleblower.

George Orwell

Bob Lazaar and Dr. Dan Burisch could be considered a perfect example according to ufologists and conspiracy's theorists.
However, in some particular instances, several an-unperson types have claimed that they have earned bona fide academic degrees in a field related to work they have done at a government's facility.

11

Dr. Dan Burisch   Bob Lazar

However, based upon meticulous investigations of their education backgound, those persons were found to be untruthful, and their degrees/diplomas and credentials were granted by unrecognized institutions.

Ancient aliens/ancient astronauts' theorists: A group of bizarre people with bizarre ideas, not to be taken seriously.
Their idiotic hypotheses and childish claims have seriously and permanently damaged ufology, and the serious work of honest researchers and authors in the field. And because they couldn't read and understand the Mesopotamian cuneiform tablets written in Sumerian, Akkadian, and Assyrian, ancient aliens and ancient astronauts' theorists fabricated stories about the Anunnaki, ancient civilizations of the Middle East, Near East, Anatolia and consequently claimed that all the majestic edifices of ancient history, the great deeds and accomplishments of our ancestors were the product of extraterrestrials.
Their so-called and bogus translations of the Mesopotamian cuneiform texts revealed their unfamiliarity with the languages of

12

the ancient world, and art history.

Even their translation/defintion of the word "Anunnaki" are outrageously wrong, for they defined Anunnaki as: "Those who from heaven to earth came" or "Those who came to earth from above." These definitions are absolutely wrong.

The Akkadian word Anunnaki is composed of two words:

a-Anunna, which means the entirety of the gods (All the gods and goddesses of Mesopotamia).

b-Ki, which means Earth, and the underworld, the netherworld, and the world of death.

Thus, the correct definition of the word Anunnnaki is: Gods of Earth and/or gods of the underworld.

The Akkadian/Sumerian Anunnaki word is used in a plural form to represent the deities of heaven and Earth, called Anunna in Sumerian and Akkadian.

Later on in history, and in order to differentiate between the Anunnaki and the Igigi, the scribes called the Anunnaki, the gods of Earth (Ki), also gods of the netherworld, and the Igigi, gods of heaven.

This differentiation is very clear in all the Mesopotamian clay tablets, particularly in the Ishtar Descent to the Underworld (Ki), the poem/myth of Gilgamesh, the Enuma Elish, etc...

Thus their definition of the Anunnaki as "Those who from heaven to earth came" is an absolute nonsense!

Samples of some of their outrageous and embarrasing claims:

1-They claim that Stonehenge (Site and stones) were built by ancient aliens as a station to refuel their UFOs! You probably heard this on their TV show.

2-They claim that Atlantis was not a continent but a huge alien spacecraft...it did not sink but flew away!!! You probably heard this on their TV show.

3-They claim that Queen Elizabeth, President George W. Bush, Prince Charles, and Hilary Clinton are reptilians!

4-They claim that ancient aliens came to Earth to mine gold, and later on to use it to patch the atmosphere of Nibiru, in order to save their planet from a cosmic catastrophe!

And to add alarming insult to injury, they claim that it was written in the Sumerian tablets. No where in any Sumerian, Akkadian, Babylonian or Assyrian tablet, such a claim exists!

More on this subject in item #23.

5-They claim that ancient aliens/ancient astronauts bombarded Earth with atomic rockets and missiles called Shumu as mentioned in the Sumerian tablets.

First, no such claim exists anywhere in the Sumerian, Akkadian, and Assyrian tablets. It is their own fabrication and a disgraceful lie.

Second, because they could not read or understand Sumerian and Akkadian, little did they know that the words Shumu and/or Shamu in Assyrian and Sumerian do not mean rocket or missiles at all.

The word Shamu in Akkadian, Assyrian, and Sumerian means:

a-The sky.

b-The heaven.

Samamu (Shamanu) in Akkadian.

Samuu (Shamuu) in Akkadian.

Samamu (Shamanu) in Assyrian.

Shmayya in contemporary Assyrian Eastern dialect.

Shayo in contemporary Assyrian Western dialect.

Sama in Arabic.

Shama in Phoenician.

Sham in Phoenician.

Sham in Ugaritic.

Shamu in Ugaritic.

Cennet in Turkish.

Sema in Turkish.

Shamu (Šamu) and Shumu ((Šumu) in Akkadian, Sumerian, and Assyrian also means: A name.

Shim in Syriac.

Shim in Chaldean.

Shumu (Šumu) in Sumerian.

Shumu (Šumu) in Akkadian.

Shumu (Šumu) in Ugaritic.

Sham in Hebrew.

Ism in Arabic.

Ismu in Arabic.
Esm in Farsi (Persian).
Shmu in Phoenician.
Isim in Turkish.
Not to confound it with the Akkadian, Assyrian, Arabic, Turkish, Ugaritic, Phoenician, and Sumerian words:
Sumerian word Shamu (Šamu).
Shmaya, in contemporary Assyrian Eastern dialect.
Shayo in contemporary Assyrian Western dialect.
Shmo in contemporary Assyrian Western dialect.
Sama in Arabic.
Sema in Turkish.
Shama and Sham in Phoenician.
Sham and Cham'u in Ugaritic.
Shamau in Akkadian.
And Shamau in Assyrian which mean sky, and heaven.
Shamu (Šamu) in Akkadian, Sumerian, and Assyrian also means: Fame, reputation, and a reference made to location (s) of cities, districts, and provinces.
6-They claim that the "saucers" Mr. Kenneth Arnold saw flying over Mount Rainier in the Cascades, in Washington State were aliens' UFOs. What Arnold saw was a formation of the German Horten 229.
7-They claim that the Nazca lines in Peru are runways for extraterrestrial and alien UFOs.
Well, the anti-gravity flying machines and spacecrafts of highly advanced civilizations don't need runways. They can land and take off vertically. Besides, those Nazcas lines are less than three feet wide. How could an extraterrestrial spaceship possibly land on a 3 foot-wide runway?
Do you honestly believe that extremely advanced extraterrestrial civilizations need miles upon miles of landing areas bordered by 2 lines and/or a runway to land their spaceships?
Are the aliens still flying DC 3 or DC 4 airplanes?
How about vertical landing and take-off? This should be a child's game to extraterrestrials!
Why do they need miles upon miles of landing runways to land their crafts?

Have you seen military jets landing on an aircraft carrier?
How long is an aircraft carrier?
The Nimitz-class super carriers have an overall length of 1092 ft
(333 meters); enough length (Lines-length) for a super jet fighter
to land and take off. So why do the aliens and ancient astronauts
need thousands of miles to land their spacecrafts?
Are we more advanced than the aliens?

Nimitz CVN-68 aircraft carrier with an overall length of 1092 ft
(333 meters).

Others have claimed that those lines were made by aliens to mark
their landing spots, so next time when they return to Earth, they
will not get lost!!
Maybe some of the ancient aliens' theorists should make it easier
on the aliens to find their way around, and give each one of them
a Radio Shack GPS (Global Positioning System) gadget.
The Nazca lines are simply a map for underground water supplies
and scattered wells, similar to thousand of wells found in Bolivia,
Chile, Guatemala, Mexico, Syria, Bahrain and Lebanon.

And this was confirmed by scientists, biologists, mineralogists, and archeologists who have studied the Nazca lines located over the underground water reservoirs. Other lines and drawings were of a religious ritual nature, as simple as that. They were created by the inhabitants of the region between 210 B.C. and 650 A.D. There are numerous Nazca geoglyphs-lines types in various areas in South America (Paraguay, Chile and Bolivia).

Cubist artists since 1909 in Russia and France used lots of circles and Nazca lines types in their compositions, yet none of them claimed that their circles were ancient aliens' helmets, and their lines were runways for their gods and muses from outer-space!!!

The pampas Nazca Lines.
No relation whatsoever to extraterrestrials!!

Some ancient astronauts, and ancient aliens' theorists claimed that these lines were made by extraterrestrials, either as part of their spacecrafts runway, or "Positioning System Marking", so they would easily recognize and/or remember where they have landed previously.

Have you ever seen any airport's runway like these overlapping lines? What would happen to airplanes if they had to use such runways? No airplane on earth will ever fly again!!The Nazca Lines are not made by extraterrestrials as claimed by ancient aliens' theorists. They are simply a net-map for underground water supplies, and other lines are of a religious (Ritual) nature, as confirmed by archeologists, scientists, and scholars.

8-They claim that the drawings of lines above the skulls of cavemen, found on the walls of prehistoric caves represent the antennas (antennae) of extraterrestrial visitors.

9-They claim that the Egyptian drawing of a triangular object topped with the beak of a bird represents an alien airplane.

10-They claim that the Pit of Oak Island is where the Ark of Covenant is hidden by aliens and their cronies.

11-They claim that the Holy Grail is hidden in the basement (the underground) of Rosslyn Chapel.

The interior of Rosslyn Chapel.

Some ufologists and 99.99% of ancient astronauts and ancient aliens theorists claim that the Knights Templar hid the Holy Grail, and other extraterrestrial treasures (Knowledge and objects) in the basement, the underground or the foundation of the Chapel. These are wild and silly assumptions.

Excavations of the Rosslyn Chapel site in the 19th century, as well as recent excavations carried out by Niven St Clair using very advanced fibre optic cameras, and a series of holes drilling beneath the chapel did not find any extraterrestrial link, a Holy Grail, or hidden treasures left by aliens. A short documentary film was made about the scientific excavations. Bottom line: No Holy Grail, no aliens' remains and no extraterrestrial link!

12-They claim that Pharaohs who had deformity in their skulls (Elongated skulls, elongated heads, so on) are alien gods because they had elongated skulls which resembled the skulls of the Grays and the little green men!!

Pharaoh Amenhotep IV.

Amenhotep IV, also known as Akhenaton and Akhenaten was baptized an alien pharaoh by ancient aliens and ancient astronauts' theorists, simply because he had an elongated skull!! They attributed the skull (Head) deformation to his divine (Royal) extraterrestrial status (Rank, authority).

Ironically, archeologists in Siberia have found several elongated skulls from the 4th century A.D., and none belonged to a king or to an alien.

Queen Nefertiti's statue showing an elongated skull.
Her elongated skull does not make her an extraterrestrial.

Drawings of people with elongated skulls and disproportionately large heads were found on the 70 million year old South America's "Iki" plates or stones. And none of them belonged to a royal, divine or extraterrestrial heritage.

Another famous elongated skull was the Pyatigorsk skull which was found during the excavation of Khasaot burial site nearby Kislovodsk.

Vladimir Kuznetsov, PhD. in historical sciences, a world authority in the field and prominent author of many books about the history and archeology of the North Caucasus said, "The skull is part of the culture of the ancient Alani.

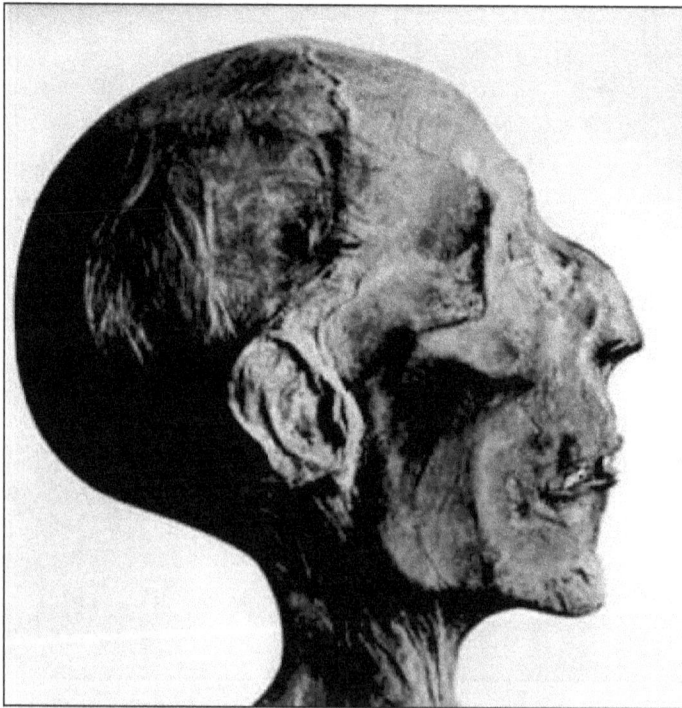

Rameses II elongated skull. He was human, not an alien.

It dates back to the 3rd – 5th centuries A.D.

These strange skulls appeared at the same time when the Sarmatian and Alani hordes came around. Some of the nomads moved for the North Caucasus in 15th century." Those "dead" folks were nomads and not divine/extraterrestrial kings.

A great number of elongated skulls of peasants and nomads was discovered by Russian archeologists. Scientists clearly stated that these elongations were a "biological response", and a "cranial deformation", and were not caused by a divine or extraterrestrial intervention.

But the ancient astronauts and ancient aliens theorists, as well as many ufologists' claim that "the ancients wanted to look aliens", and/or were aliens-humans hybrids, or even real aliens, like the Pharaoh Tutankhamun and Queen Nefertiti.

Southern Malakula's Ambat also had an elongated head.

And the most elongated skulls were found in Tomman Island, and none of the inhabitants of that island ever heard of aliens or extraterrestrials.

In the megalithic temple of Hal Saflienti located in Malta, we found the remains of people with a huge cranial deformation.

13-They claim that SS Nazi officers are extraterrestrials disguised as humans in German military uniforms.

14-They claim that Queen Elizabeth II, and our former President George W. Bush are reptilians, and suck people's blood in secret macabre ritual ceremonies.

15-They claim that Zetas and small gray aliens creatures are invading people's apartments in Manhattan, swamps in Louisiana and cowboys bars, abducting them, lifting them up in the air like sacs of potatoes and throwing them on surgical tables inside UFOs and stuffing their bodies with alien devices, and instructing them to go preach the celestial alien message of love and hope to humanity.

16-They claim that extraterrestrials eat humans' flesh and drink animals' blood.

17-They claim that circles drawn around the heads of prehistoric figures, cavemen and ancient people on caves' walls represent astronauts' helmets from outer-space.

18-They claim that Nibiru is the 12th Planet! No, it is not!
The Anunnaki (Anu.Na.Ki) and their offspring (2 categories/2 classes) came to Earth from Ash.Ta.Ri (Aldebaran) constellation as exactly Maria Orsic, the Anunnaki Ulema have said, and as mentioned in various archaic Middle Eastern and Near Eastern inscriptions. Is there any passage, any line, any reference in the Enuma Elish "Epic of Creation", the "Epic of Gilgamesh", and/or any Akkadian/Sumerian clay tablets, mentioning Nibiru as the 12th planet? None whatsoever!
There are no records to that effect in the ancient Assyrian, Akkadian, Sumerian, Babylonian and Mesopotamian texts.
The Akkadian/Sumerian scribes used the word Nibiru, more correctly Ne.Be.Ru as a name for Jupiter, and later on, referred to Mercury as Nibiru.
Even their god, the mighty Anunnaki Marduk was called Nibiru.
Where do we find the word Nibiru (Ne.Be.Ru) in the Sumerian, Akkadian and Assyrian Tablets?
1-In the Epic of Enuma Elish, Tablet 7, Lines 124, 125
Akkadian/Sumerian text (Transliteration):
d Ne.be.ru ne.be.re-et same, u erseti lu tamehma
Translation:
Let him be the holder of the crossing of heavens and earth.
Note: "*Let him*" means Nibiru and Marduk.
And Mercury and Jupiter were associated with god Marduk.
This is documented in the epic of "Enuma Elish", in Tablet VII, lines: 126,130,131.
It is also translated by some Assyriologists as follows:
Let Nibiru be the marker "Holder" of
Heaven and earth crossing place.
Note: "Same" (Pronounced Shameh) means heaven.
Sama in Arabic. Shem in Phoenician, Shama in Ulemite.
Shamayim in Hebrew; a plural form meaning heights.
"erseti" means Earth. Other words: Ersetu, Erdsetu.
Erd (Ard) in Arabic. Heretz (Eretz) in Hebrew. Erda in Ulemite.

2. Neberu also appeared in lines 130 and 131.
Akkadian/Sumerian text (Transliteration):
d Ne.be.ru kakkabu- su

24

sa ina same usupuu
Translation:
"Ne.Be.Ru is *his star,* which he made appear in the heavens."
Also translated as follows: "Nibiru is *his* star which in
heavens made it appear."
Note: "*His star*" refers to Marduk.

3. Also in the Epic of Enuma Elish, Tablet 5, Line 6.
Here is the text:
usarsid man-zadaz
d Ne.Be.Ru ana uddu-urik-si-suun
Translation:
He promptly set the position (Place) of
Nibiru to fix *their* limits (Frontiers, boundaries).
Or
He created the station of
Nibiru to determine *their* bounds.
Note:
He, refers to Markuk.
Their, refers to planets or stars.
Interesting information in the following lines:
8. He (Marduk) fixed the station of Bel and Ea along with him.
9. He opened great gates (Ba'abs) on both sides.

4. In Tablet 7, Line 109.
Let *his name* be Nibiru, the capturer of the midst.
Note: *His name,* means Marduk.
Also in Tablet 7, Line 126.
Translation of the Akkadian/Sumerian text: "The stars of heaven,
let him set their course; *let him* shepherd all the gods like sheep."
Note: "*Let him*" refers to Ne.Be.Ru.

In the Sumerian/Akkadian texts, we found this line:
"Nebarti Asshur."
Meaning: "The Crossing Point of Asshur."
Note: Asshur "Assur" was an ancient Mesopotamian-Babylonian-
Assyrian city.
In another passage, we found this line:

"ina Abani nibiru uchaduu."
Meaning: To "have cut off the crossing way of the river Abani."
Note: This passage refers to the Elamites.
Reference: The Epic of Gilgamesh.
Text from the Epic: "Straight is the crossing point, and narrow is the way that leads to it."

The Akkadian and Sumerian word Ne.Bi.Rim means crossing.
Akkadian/Sumerian text (Transliteration):
shiqil kaspum sha ne.bi.rim.
Translation: Silver paid for the crossing.
Meaning: A fee was paid for a person who transports people, across the waters.
Ne.bi.rim as a word, means crossing.
Nebiri as a verb, means to cross something or cross over.

In 1902, L.W. King provided us with the following translation of Tablets 5 and 7 of the Enuma Elish "Epic of the Creation":

In the Fifth Tablet we read:
He (Marduk) made the stations for the great gods;
The stars, their images, as the stars of the Zodiac, he fixed.
He ordained the year and into sections he divided it;
For the twelve months he fixed three stars.
After he had ... the days of the year ... images,
He founded the station of *Nibiru (the planet Jupiter)* to determine their bounds;
That none might err or go astray,
He set the station of Bel and Ea along with him.
He opened great gates on both sides,
He made strong the bolt on the left and on the right.
In the midst thereof he fixed the zenith;
The Moon-god he caused to shine forth, the night he entrusted to him.
He appointed him, a being of the night, to determine the days;
In the Seventh Tablet, we read:
He (Marduk) named the four quarters of the world, mankind he created,

The Creator of the earth.
May he hold the Beginning and the Future, may they pay homage unto him,
Saying, "He who forced his way through the midst of Tiamat without resting,
Let his *name (Marduk)* be *Nibiru,* "the Seizer of the Midst!"
For the stars of heaven he upheld the paths,
He shepherded all the gods like sheep!
He conquered Tiamat,
he troubled and ended her life,"
In the future of mankind,
when the days grow old,
May this be heard without ceasing;
may it hold sway forever!
Since he created the realm of heaven
and fashioned the firm earth.

Mul.Apin:
Here is the text (Transliteration):
Kima kakka-bu sut *d*Enlil ugdammiruni isten kakkabu
Rabu sessu da mat same ustamsalma izzaz kakkab
D Amar.Ud Ne.Be.Ru sagme. gar mamzassu
Ittanakkir same ibbir
Translation:
When the stars of Enlil were completed (Finished)
One star with big dim light, he (Enlil) divides the heaven (Sky) in half and stands there
That is the star (of Marduk) Ne.Be.Ru Jupiter which keeps Changing its position and traverses the Heaven (Sky).
Note: The last two lines: sagme.gar mamzassu Ittanakkir same ibbir. The text seems to tell us that Nibiru did cross the sky! Is it a contradiction, or simply, the two lines meant that Nibiru was rotating around another star? The Akkadian/Sumerian texts do not provide any explanation. The Anunnaki and the Anunnaki Ulema identified Aldebran (Ash.Ta.Ri) as their constellation, and Ne.Be.Ru as a crossing point to other dimensions.
Epistemologically the Arabic words of "Aldebaran", "Abirun", the Arabic verbs, "Abara", "Abra", the Sumerian and Akkadian word

27

"Ne.bi.rim", and the Ana'kh/Ulemite words "Ashtari Aldebaran barazat Ne.Be.Ru" refer in essence to the very same thing:
Aldebaran (The Constellation of Ashtari) home of Maria Orsic Alderbaran's extraterrestrials and Anunnaki.
19-They claim that the Mayan sculpture in Tikal, Guatemala represents an alien astronaut. They claim that this sculpture (shown below) is a depiction of an astronaut wearing a space helmet.
They are wrong.
Check ancient Phoenician art found in Tyre (modern day Sour), Sidon (modern day Saida), Byblos (modern day Jbeil), Ugarit and Amrit artifacts, Carthaginian statues and figurines, plates and slabs from Dilmun (modern day Bahrain), and you will find plenty of similar artifacts.

A Mayan sculpture in Tikal, Guatemala.
This is not an ancient astronaut's helmet, but an ornamental hat used in ritual ceremonies. Even Native Americans and several African tribes used almost identical so-called helmet!!

The sarcophagus or coffin of K'inich Janahb Pakal, circa 603-683 AD, discovered in the Temple of Inscriptions in Mexico, 1952.

20-They claim that the Mayan sarcophagus or coffin of K'inich Janahb Pakal, depicts an ancient astronaut flying an extraterrestrial rocket.

The truth is this: The original illustration of the sarcophagus (Which was doctored by them) represents Pascal, a Mayan ruler with the Quetzal bird. They intentionally camouflaged the bird to hide the true meaning, which is a scene of a Mayan ruler with Quetzal bird situated between two worlds; the world of the afterlife, and the world of the living.

This scene represents the rising of the Sun God suspended on a cross made from corn plants, which to the Mayan people meant fertility. But because they were unable to read pertinent Mayan inscriptions, and because they are not familiar with the history of traditions and religious symbols of the Mayans, they interpreted Pascal as an alien pilot and the cross as an extraterrestrial UFO!!

21-They claim that the Eastern Island monolithic stones were carved and moved by ancient aliens.

Ancient astronauts' theorists claim that the inhabitants of the island did not have the means or the technology to transport these massive stones. And the people who lived there, centuries ago, did not have wood and ropes needed for the construction and transportation of the statues. Their claims show their lack of knowledge of the ancient history of the island.

Archaeology and history of the island tell us that the island was covered with trees, but unfortunately they were totally cut to make room for agriculture. And the inhabitants were capable of cutting and transporting those massive statues.

In fact, in 1955, Norwegian explorer, Thor Heyerdahl saw with his own eyes how natives of the island used archaic tools to cut new statues of the same size, and how only 180 men moved one huge statue to its destined place without any problem; they used different kinds of ropes to drag the massive statue.

And it required only 12 men to elevate the statue using round and rectangular rocks and strong wooden legs.

It took them only 11 months to complete the whole project.

Eastern Island monolithic stone statue (Mo'ai of Rapa Nui).

22-Spheres, clouds, circles and globes in medieval religious art, Renaissance art and classic Italian paintings are UFOS!

31

Ancient aliens, ancient astronauts theorists, numerous ufologists, and thousands of ignorami who post all sorts of things on their UFOs websites, without any familiarity with classic painting and art history insist that the symbolic and religious motifs such as a dove, a fish, a circle of light, and globes (which are a metaphoric expression of the Church) ARE aliens' spaceships!!
I wrote extensively on the subject.
Please read on the next pages a scanned article of mine published in "Art, UFOs and Supernatural Magazine". And please pay attention to enlarged sections of classical and religious paintings, which are the center of their claims.
The article has a strong emphasis on: Their total ignorance of art history, meaning of symbolism in the early Christian Church, how a cardinal's hat was interpreted as a UFO, The Annunciation painting by Crivelli, and The Eucharist Painting by Salimbeni.

*** *** ***

A Cardinal's hat becomes a UFO!!

Look at the painting on the left.

Many ufologists and almost all ancient aliens and ancient astronauts theorists claim that what you see on the lower right side of this painting is a UFO. They are wrong.

They are mistaken because they are not familiar with the early religious (Catholic) arts, and especially the various phases of the Italian religious art, and the frescos of the Vatican.

So, let me prove to you step-by-step, how ignorant they are. First, let's talk about this painting. It is called "Scene di vita eremitica" (Scene of hermitic life), by Paolo Uccello.

The painting you are looking at is an enlarged section taken from the original painting of Uccello.

See full size of the painting below.
"Scene of hermitic life", by Paolo Uccello.

Section taken from the painting.
This enlarged section, always from the same painting reveals that the red circular object on the lower right is not a UFO, but simply the hat of a Roman Catholic Cardinal.

Left: The person who is kneeling before Jesus on the cross is St. Jerome, himself a Cardinal.

St. Jerome renounced his title as Cardinal and relinquished all the powers and privileges bestowed upon him and his title by becoming a hermit. This fact is documented by the Vatican as well as in books on the history of St. Jerome and a multitude of books and writings on the saints of the Catholic Church.

St. Jerome's renunciation is clearly depicted by the red hat of a Cardinal thrown on the floor as illustrated in the painting. And has nothing to do with an extraterrestrial UFO!! The theme of St. Jerome's renunciation was also depicted in several paintings by other Masters of the religious Roman Italian art in the 16th and 17th centuries, and was visibly illustrated in famous paintings by Agnolo Bronzino, Benozzo Gozzoli and Albrecht Dürer.

Another religious painting of St. Jerome after he has renounced his title as a Roman Cardinal. His red Cardinal hat appears on the lower right side of the painting.

Ancient astronauts theorists who did not study Italian religious art and the history of the early Roman Saints interpret the Cardinal's red hat as an alien UFO!!

From left to right: 1-Enlarged section representing the red hat of a Roman Catholic Cardinal; the very same hat St Jerome's wore when he was a Roman Cardinal. As you can see, there is no UFO here!! 2- Painting of "St. Jerome in the Wilderness", by Albrecht Dürer,1495.

The same red circular red hat of a Roman Cardinal (Lower left side of the painting) was painted in numerous paintings to remind us of St. Jerome's renunciation of his position as a Cardinal and his decision to become a hermit.

Left: In the eyes of ancient astronauts theorists and ancient aliens theorists, the hat of a Cardinal becomes an extraterrestrial UFO!! Photo credit: ETC/FCIT.

The "Annunciation" Painting" by Crivelli

The Annunciation" by Carlo Crivelli.

Now we look at a painting "The Annunciation" by Carlo Crivelli (left) that was aggressively used by some ufologists, ancient aliens theorists and ancient astronauts theorists to back up their claims that UFOs did appear in ancient religious art. Basically what they did with this painting was reproducing it on their websites and TV shows in an unclear manner, meaning you could not really see what they were talking about. But all those who saw the original painting in a museum could not see any UFO in the painting.

But when the theorists mentioned above published a photo of the painting, intentionally they did not show you an enlarged photo of the whole painting, in order to hide the truth from you. What you see in the ancient aliens and ancients astronauts' theorists reproduction of the original painting is a distortion of the truth, and I am going to prove it to you. They claim that the circular object painted on the upper left side of the painting is a UFO, an alien spaceship.

But when we enlarge the photo of the original painting, or if you are looking at the painting in a museum, you will find out that this object is not UFO at all. So, let's enlarge the photo of the painting, and find out.

Left: Enlarged section from the original painting. Enlargement of the section containing the so-called UFO. It is not a UFO but a circle of angels with divine rays.

The rays or light emanating from a circle was a visual illustration of divinity in Byzantine Art, early Christian illustrations, Roman art and the Renaissance art.

But in the eyes of ancient astronauts and ancient aliens theorists, this religious illustration is simply a UFO. Yah right, they know better than the artists who painted these masterpieces and the historians of art. This illustration of a circle of light was very common in the work of the Masters throughout the centuries, encompassing the artists of the Armenian Illuminated Manuscripts, the painters of the early epochs of Byzantium art, the Coptic calligraphers and painters, Renaissance Masters, the Syriac scribes and illustrators, etc. Those who have studied Byzantine art would understand what a circle of light means. Historians, experts and students of the arts (painting and architecture) of the Christian era of Constantinople know very well that a circle of light, or an oval form of clouds and lights represent the "Divine Source", "Divinity", and God. In many instances, those circles contained the faces of angels, and were surrounded by bright rays representing the celestial nature of the message.

37

See on the next page an enlargement of the circle emanating a beam, ancient astronauts and some ufologists interpreted it as a UFO!!

This is not a UFO! But a sphere of divine light/rings of angels! It is simply two circles of angels inside a cloud.

The Eucharist Painting of Salimbeni.
Ancient aliens and ancient astronauts' theorists claimed that the globe in the center of this painting is a UFO with 2 antennas (antennae).

They are wrong as usual. Let's blow up the picture and see what we can find out. See next pages, with a pertinent explanation.

Explanation:
The globe is not a UFO, but the terrestrial globe, representing the Creation. And the two rods are not UFOs' antennas (antennae), but rather the Divine Scepters of the Holy Trinity, and God/Jesus authority over the world.

23-They claim that the extraterrestrials (ancient aliens and ancient astronauts) created men (The human race) as slaves in order to mine gold for them, as it was written in the Sumerian tablets. This is utterly false.

There is no such thing, there is absolutely no reference made to such claim in any of the Assyrian, Babylonian-Assyrian, Sumero-Akkadian, and Chaldean clay tablets!

As a linguist who wrote more than 60 books in the field, and 43 volumes encyclopedic dictionaries (Lexicon/Thesaurus) of the ancient languages of Mesopotamia, Asia Minor, the Near East, and the Middle East, and translated the Sumerian, Akkadian, and Assyrian cuneiform clay tablets, I can assure you that the Anunnaki (Ancient aliens/Ancient astronauts) did not create us to mine for gold.

You will find below my translations of the Sumerian, Akkadian, and Assyrian texts, and tablets, exactly as they were written by the Mesopotamian scribes. According to the ancient texts, we were created to till the land, to farm, to dig ditches, to work the fields (The lands of Mesopotamia), in order to feed the ancient gods; a hard labor which was assigned to the Igigi.

We were created to replace the Igigi! And not to mine gold.

The Mesopotamian texts contradict what ancient aliens and ancient astronauts' theorists' claim.

Here is the translation of the original Sumerian texts:
Nintu and Enki plan the creation of the human race (I: 178-220);
Enki, rather than Anu, is speaking at this time.
In these versions, Enki reveals his plan for creating the human race. Enki said:
"While Nintu the birth-goddess is here,
let her create the offspring...
let man carry the basket of labor of the Anunna (gods)."

Enki and Nintu called the goddess and said to her:
"You are the goddess of birth
and the creator of man.
Create for the Gods, the Lulu (man),

Let him bear the yoke,
let Lulu carry the basket of labor
of the Anunna. "

Important note: The Anunnaki did not come to Earth to mine gold. The Sumero-Akkadian phrase on the Sumerian tablet: *"the labor-basket of the gods"* means that first humans were created to work the fields and feed the Anuna (Gods), fill up the basket of food, fruits and cereals, and not to mine for gold.

Geshtu-e: The slaughtered Igigi god and the creation of the "First Man".

Geshtu-e is the Akkadian/Sumerian name of the Igigi god whose blood and intelligence were used by the Anunnaki Mami to create the first man.

In the beginning, before men were created, the Anunnaki, (the extraterrestrial gods living on planet Earth), had to till the land and water it to grow their food. And this was hard and extremely demanding labor.

Enlil summoned the Igigi, and asked them to do the job.

The Igigi's revolt:

In addition to cultivating and working the fields in ancient Iraq (Babylon, Sumer), Enlil assigned to the Igigi, the hard tasks of digging trenches, canals, and river beds.

And the Igigi kept on doing this hard labor for centuries, until they could not take it anymore.

They threw down their tools and went en masse to Ekur, Enlil's citadel at Nippur, to protest this hardship, and to demand immediate relief.

When the Igigi reached the citadel, Enlil ordered Nusku, his doorkeeper, to keep them out of Ekur.

Nusku asked Enlil:

"Why do you fear your sons?
Call the other gods and let t
hem help solve this thing."

So Enlil summoned the gods, including Anu and Enki.
Together, they rushed to help Enlil, and stood firm on the
ramparts of the citadel, and spoke to the furious Igigi:
"Why are you attacking us?
And the Igigi answered:
"The work you have assigned to us is killing us;
we can no longer bear it.
We have stopped digging the trenches
and we are declaring war."

Enki asked the gods for advice, and said to them:
"Why do we blame the Igigi?
Their tasks are too hard.
Goddess Mami is with us.
Let her create human beings to serve us
and to do the work of the Igigi.
So we can put the yoke
of Enlil on these creatures
and let the Igigi return to heaven."

The Anunnaki decided to create humans:
The gods agreed, and asked goddess Mami to create beings to do
the work of the Igigi, not to mine for gold.
Mami said:
"It is not wise for me to do all this.
You should choose Enki instead,
because he is wise and does things right.
But if he prepares the clay needed
to complete the task,
I will create these beings."

Enki replied:
"If we use only clay to create new beings,
they will be like animals, without intelligence.
Instead, we must slaughter one of the gods,
to make these creatures capable
of bearing Enlil's yoke.
We can mix his flesh and blood

with clay to create a Man."

The Anunnaki seized Geshtu-e, and slaughtered him:
The Anunnaki seized Geshtu-e, the Igigi god of wisdom and knowledge, and slaughtered him. As soon as his flesh and blood were mixed with the clay, a Shabbah (Ghost) manifested, and took the shape of a human being.
Mami seized the ghost, and divided him into fourteen pieces, to create seven females and seven males. These creatures were the first prototypes of the human race.

Mami presented her creatures to the Anunnaki, and said:
"I have done everything you have asked.
I have created Man (Men and Women).
And I gave them the faculty of speaking,
so they could talk to each other
and do the job.
Let each Man choose a wife.
And Ishtar will bless them
with healthy children,
to fill the whole Earth
with generations of servants."

Note: This is why and how Man was created by the Anunnaki at that time in history. Humans were created to do the Igigi's hard labor in the fields, and to feed the Anunnaki. And not to mine gold as erroneously claimed by ancient astronauts and ancient aliens theorists, and famous authors in the West!!

The Mesopotamian cuneiform tablets never ever mentioned that the Anunnaki came to planet Earth to mine for gold, or they created humans to mine for gold either!
The Mesopotamian tablets made it clear to us that the Anunnaki created mankind to replace the Igigi who complained constantly because of the heavy agricultural work which included working the fields, digging waters' canals, irrigation, planting, harvesting, feeding the gods, and an avalanche of other hard physical works at Nippur, the Anunnaki imposed upon them for many years.

46

Andrews Air Force Base: Ufologists and conspiracy theorists claim that Andrews is the base where the dead bodies of the aliens of a UFO which crashed in Lincoln County, approximately 75 miles NW of Roswell were taken to, on Monday July 7, 1947, and stoted in Hangar 18 of the base. Others added that Hangar 18 also store the UFO's debris and wreckage.

AAFB Flight line.

Lt. Colonel Philip J. Corso claimed that he opened one of the boxes (trunks) which were transported to Wright Patterson and saw an alien body, three to four 4 foot tall, preserved in blue liquid.

Anfeh: The name of an old town in Lebanon. Anfeh's history goes back to the time of the Phoenicians/Canaanites. Its ancient name is Ambi, and it was mentioned in Tel-El-Amarina letters, in the 14th century B.C., as well as in the Assyrian inscriptions of King Asr-Hadoun (681-669 B.C.)

47

In the 12th century, Anfeh was called Nafin by the Crusaders. Anfeh is known for its historic Citadel of Anfeh which is located on a small peninsula called Raas Anfeh. This citadel was used by the Crusaders and Knights Templar as an esoteric center, where ancient Ana'kh manuscripts and King Solomon's Testament were read regularly. On the north side of Anfeh, the Crusaders built an underground base for their secret esoteric meetings. Saint Jean de Luz was the master of ceremonies.

Legend has it that Anfeh was one of the earliest Anunnaki landing areas in the Near East. The Book of Rama Dosh tells us that at Anfeh, the Anunnaki established a medical cente, for advanced genetic experiments. Anfeh, and the island of Arwad shared a very advanced genetic program, designed to experiment with DNA of the primitive humans who lived in the Near and the Middle East.

The Citadel of Anfeh, built by the Crusaders.

Anfeh, Lebanon.

Old Anfeh.

Angel Hair: A term for a substance resembling gelatin or jelly, allegedly created from inonized air, which has an electromagnetic property, and surround a UFO.

This term was popularized by Raelism. Some have claimed that Angel Hair is a physical manifestation of ectoplasma which occurs in apparition of saints and superbeings. According to Pravda, "Angel hais is a cobweb-like and jellylike substance which is also slightly radioactive often falls to the ground shortly after UFO sightings. The substance dubbed "angel's hair" evaporates without a trace several hours after the sighting. The "hair" was reported to either disintegrate or turn into cottony tufts with an offensive smell when held in the hand.

American ufologists refer to the material as "angel's hair"; Italians call it "siliceous cotton"; and the French use the term "The Madonna's present" to describe semitransparent threads that fall from heavens."

Angel radar: A term commonly used by operators of radar to refer to a radar echo of natural phenomena such as a tornado or birds' flocks, and which is totally unrelated to UFOs.

However, ufologists claim that angel radar is a heavy and fibrous substance usually observed around a trail made by a UFO. Others referred angel radar to a greyish substance produced by by an USO or a USO upon submerging underwater.

This claim is totally incorrect, for USOs or UFOs upon entering or "ditching" into the sea, do not touch the surface of the water, and do not leave any trace behind them, since they create a "Vacuum Vortex" in front of the craft, which expands to the rear of the flying machine once the body of the craft is totally submerged.

Angelic Stone: Name of a stone allegedly used by John Dee, a medium and astrologer of Queen Elizabeth I, who claimed that the stone was given to him by angel Gabriel and angel Raphael.

Dee stated that the stone was also a tool he used to communicate with celestial extraterrestrials who provided him with a wealth of information on the secret of life, the divine origin of man, the true nature of God, and a detailed description of beings of lights from

John Dee

a higher dimension. The Angelic Stone is on display at the British Museum. Dee also claimed that the extraterrestrials gave him the power to summon the dead and foresee the future.

Many dignitaries of Queen Elizabeth I Court believed in him.

The Angelic Stones of John Dee on display at the British Museum.

Animal mutilation: It refers to particular cases where animals (cows/cattle) were found dead due to injuries of a circular shape done with a surgical precision, and the corpse of the animal is totally drained of blood. A series of animal mutilations surfaced for the first time in 1963 in Haskell County in Texas.

52

Numerous ufologists claim that animal mutilations were caused by extraterrestrials using some sort of laser beams, and that short after, black helicopters were seen hovering over the "crime scene", after the departure of UFOs which have caused such mutilations. Tom Adams, in an article published in Stigmata in 1978, wrote, "The helicopters are themselves UFOs, disguised to appear as terrestrial crafts."
Cattle rancher Tom Miller from Colorado said, "There are so many things about this I don't understand, and no one seems to know what is going on, or be able to explain it. First, I thought the cow died from natural cause, you know...naturally, and then I got closer to the cow, and I saw it wasn't natural...The eyes were gone, no tongue, no ears, and sex organs were cut out."

Author Nick Redfern stated that some UFO theorists strongly believe that extraterrestrials are using the blood of cows for hybrid fertilization. Many authors disagree.
Chris O'Brien, who conducted numerous and extensive research and investigations about animal mutilation, mocked ufologists' theory.
He wondered why would some highly advanced civilizations who travelled light years come to earth to kill animals and collect their bodies'parts. It just doesn't make sense.
It is his belief that the mutilations are conducted by a secret agency which is monitoring the food chain "to prevent another outbreak of Bovine Spongiform Encephalopathy that plagued Great Britain in 1996."

Animated entities: This misinterpreted expression entered both ufology's literature and realm of religious apparitions, for it encompasses a multitude of entities of complex structures and undefined organisms, as well as inexplicable religious apparitions, and psychosomatic manifestations.
For example, the apparition of the Virgin Mary of Fatima is considered a typical animated entity. And Dr. Hynek's personal classification of animated entities included unidentified flying discs.

Dr. J. Allen Hynek

In ufology, humanoids are also defined as animated entities. Dr. J. Allen Hynek's classifications included lights in the sky, discs, saucers, crafts without visible propulsion system, cigar-shaped crafts, triangular lights, spheres, domes and orbs. Hynek classified three distant sightings/animated entities as follows:

1-RV; radar-visual cases.

2-DD; daylight discs.

3-NL; nocturnal lights.

Anki: Sumerian/Akkadian. Noun. The universe.
Composed of two words:
a- An, which meanch sky; God; the origin,
b- Ki, which means the Earth.
Ki also means the underworld, and the world of no return. It is taken from the word Kurnugi, which means hell, and the empire of death. Ki is referred to as the "Land of no return" in the Akkadian clay tablets.

54

Anomalous aerial phenomena: A term used by Dr. Jacques Vallee et al to explain and group incidents or observations derived from a multitude of factors such:
1-Physical manifestations.
2-Psychological factors.
3-Psychosomatic effects.
4-Anti-physical effects.
5-Physiological factors.
6-Psychic effects.
7-Cultural effects.

Dr. Jacques Vallee

Anomalous propagation: Also called AP radar. A term used to explain that waves emitted by a radar can in some particular instances propagate differently than the anticipated straight line, caused by layers of air and strong temperatures. Some ufologists have claimed that those waves were blips which registered the presence of a UFO on the radar's screen/grid.

Anshar: Sumerian. Noun. Name of the Sumerian male principal, and the god of the heaven. He was born of the serpent Lakhmu (Lakhamu).

Anshar was the father of Anu, and the son of Apsu and Tiamat. Anshar mated with his sister Kishar and created the great gods.Anshar convinced the gods to fight Tiamat.

Antarctica (Antarctic bases of German UFOs): Lt. Colonel Walter Horten, co-inventor of the German Horten 229 (Wing-craft) stated that Heinz Schaeffer, Captain of the "U-977" (German submarine) which was stationed in the Baltic Sea took Hitler, and Eva Braun to Argentina. It took them almost 2 months and 10 days to reach Argentina. They manage to escape with the help of a very powerful British Lord and the American military high command. From Argentina, they went to a military base in Antarctica. After the war, Schaeffer was recruited by the Americans.

Lt. Colonel Walter Horten and his brother Lt. Colonel Reimar Horten.

Hitler's Nazi military colony in Antarctica.
During the Second World War, Germany was sending fleets of submarines, ships, and exotic spacecrafts to their colony, the Neu Schwabenland in Antarctica, and to other secret locations and underground bases known only to Himmler, Kammler and to an elite of their military scientists.

Insiders, whistleblowers, as well as United States and British intelligence agents have confirmed that those underground secret bases were later used by the Germans after the war, as their new headquarters, and center for their anti-gravity crafts and flying discs.

Rudolf Hess in the garden of a British prison at Spandau in West Berlin.

Rudolf Hess.
In a British prison at Spandau in West Berlin, where he died in 1987, Rudolf Hess, Hitler's Deputy admitted to US military intelligence that Germany had a sophisticated and very advanced military base in Antarctica. Lindbergh told Carl Jung that the United States Air Force investigated the matter. Files upon files confiscated by the allies at the secret German bases in the Harz Mountains, Thuringia and Peenemünde referred to the Antarctic's base locations.

Rudolf Hess

The OSS and the CIA compiled lists and dossiers on highly advanced types and new classes of post-war German anti-gravity crafts/flying saucers which were built at those locations and Antarctica.

In 1950, one of the CIA's secret memoranda revealed that in fact, a highly advanced type of German flying discs and Wing-Jets seen over the United States and European countries came from the Antarctic's German new headquarters.

In 1951, the Soviet Union and the United States secretly and jointly sent two expeditions to Antarctica to spy on post-war Germany's new centers and underground facilities and factories in Neu Schwabenland (Antarctica).

The expeditions were mentioned in a secret CIA memorandum issued by General Walter Bedell Smith, then director of the CIA, and in a secret memorandum issued by Allen Welsh Dulles, then the Deputy Director of the Agency.

In addition to the immense Neu Schwabenland's base, post-war Germany's scientists also established secret factories in remote areas in Canada; this was confirmed by:

- Dr. von Braun,
- Major Erich Hartmann,
- Rudolph Schriever,
- Dr. Hermann Oberth,
- General Dr. Walter Dornberger,
- Dr. Heinrich Richard Miethe,
- Dr. Albert Kochendoerfer,
- Dr. Bruno Wolf Bruckmann,
- Robert Seamans (Associate NASA Administrator),
- Walter Haeussemann (NASA Director of Astrionics Division),
- Major General John Barclay,
- Lt. Colonels Walter and Reimar Horten,
- General Emmett "Rosie" O'Donnell, then, head of the United States Strategic Air Force Command.
- Chairman of the Joint Chiefs of Staff, General Nathan F. Twinning who revealed explosive information on the subject but was silenced.

Some powerful people in American politic and the military covered up the whole story, to name a few:

General John Samford,
General Roger Maxwell Ramey,
General Curtis LeMay,
General Hoyt S. Vandenberg,
President Harry Truman members of National Defense Research Committee which included:
Roger Adams,
Vannevar Bush,
K. T. Compton,
James Bryant Conant,
Alphonse Raymond,

Albert Baird,
Jerome Clarke,
Frank B. Jewett,
Alfred Newton,
Lewis Hill.

Admiral William James Crowe, Jr.

Admiral William James Crowe, Jr.
On two occasions, Admiral William James Crowe, Jr., Chairman of the Joint Chiefs of Staff, discussed the affair with President Ronald Reagan and Prime Minister Margaret Thatcher.
President Ronald Reagan had limited access to the government's secret files on Hitler's Nazi military colony in Antarctica.
Admiral Crowe reassured the President that the German base in Antarctica was no threat to national security. He added that President Truman and President Eisenhower had some sort of an agreement with the "old school" and remnants of Nazi scientists in Germany, Austria, Poland and Antarctica.

While serving as the U.S. ambassador to Great Britain (1994-97), the Admiral had intensive talks with Prime Minister Margaret Thatcher about the Falklands war, and of course Adolf Hitler's Antarctica base. And again, he reassured the Prime Minister that the Antarctica base is no threat to Great Britain and to the United States.

Back then, Operation Paperclip was a top secret operation. Finally, the word got out in 1972, and by 1973-1974, Operation Paperclip was declassified.

This operation was deemed necessary, and recruiting Nazi scientists was authorized by President Harry Truman. According to Major General Hugh Knerr, then, the Deputy Commander of the United States Strategic Forces in Europe, "The Germans were way ahead of us, especially in the development of weapons systems."

And based upon what he read and discovered in numerous files of the SS and the Luftwaffe, the Allies captured in Germany, General Hugh Knerr advised President Truman to "round up" Nazi scientists and "ship" them to the United States.

Lt. General Spatz.

61

He also wrote two detailed reports on Germany's rockets and "other" unidentified flying objects, which he submitted to 4 star General Carl Spaatz.

General Spaatz said to President Truman, "If we don't get the German scientists, first...the Russians will..."

General Donovan, head of the OSS warned the President that recruiting Nazi scientists is illegal.

President Truman was very concerned, and he ordered the OSS and other military intelligence units to check up on the political affiliation of those scientists, and stated very clearly that any German scientist who had a close tie to the SS and/or is a member of the Nazi party, will not be recruited and sent to America. Mr. Hoover, then Director of the FBI did a magnificent job in investigating the German scientists.

Dr. von Braun managed to convince the President that America needed those scientists whether they were Nazi or not.

Reluctantly, the President accepted, and many of the allegedly criminal records of German scientists vanished from the face of the Earth. And thus, two military intelligence units and later, the JIOA (Joint Intelligence Objectives Agency) began to establish the recruitment's procedures under the direct control of Captain Bosquet Neill Wev, then, the Director of the JIOA.

"Nazism no longer should be a serious consideration."

In a secret memo issued in April 1948, and sent to the Director of Intelligence at the Pentagon, Wev stated word for word, "Investigations conducted by the military have disclosed the fact that the majority of German scientists were members of either the Nazi Party or one or more of its affiliates."

However in mid of March 1948, Wev wrote a letter to the State Department, in which he stated the following, "Nazism no longer should be a serious consideration from a viewpoint of national security when the far greater threat of Communism is now jeopardizing the entire world."

During 1948, Wev and other high-ranking officers facilitated additional Nazi scientists' recruitments and "friendly" meetings and interviews with Germany leading scientists, such as Lt. Colonel Reimar Horten, the inventor of the Horten 229 (The Wing-Jets formation spotted by Ken Anorld over Mt. Rainier in Washington State).

Back then, everybody believed that recruiting Nazi scientists and exotic flying spacecrafts (RFC2), and the notorious Kraftstrahl Kanoen/Kraft Stahl Kanoen (Nazi Ray of Death Weapon) experts was the right thing to do. As a result, an elaborate new dossier on Antarctica' Nazi colony saw the light.

The White House, The Pentagon and the State Department were acting in the best interest of the United States, even though the investigations revealed that 98% of those German scientists were 100% Nazi.

In addition, our administration welcomed noted Nazi spies because of their impressive knowledge of the NKVD and Stalin's regime. The most notorious Nazi spy was Reinhard Gehlen.

Dr. von Braun, Head of Operation Paperclip with Nazi officers in 1941.

Below, you will find a self-explanatory document (Draft of
Captain Wev). It is authentic, and secret.

TOP SECRET

THE JOINT CHIEFS OF STAFF
Washington 25, D. C.

Joint Intelligence Objectives Agency

31 March 1948

JIOA 1068

  MEMORANDUM FOR Collection Branch, Air Intelligence
      Requirements Division

Attn: Directorate of Intelligence

SUBJECT: German Scientists (Civil), Reimar Horten.

   1. Reference is made to the recent telephone
request of Captain Macken that Dr. Reimar Horten, allocated
to the U.K. on the U.K. 15th Civil List, be made available
to the Department of the Air Force for interview.

   2. The British Joint Services Missions has agreed
to the interview of Horten by the Department of the Air
Force at some future date.

          /s/ BOSQUET N. WEV
           Captain, USN
            Director

Document from the United States War Department.
Subject: Outstanding German Scientists Being Brought to U.S.

War Department
Bureau of Public Relations
Press Branch
Tel. RE 6500
Brs. 3425 and 4660

October 1, 1945

IMMEDIATE   RELEASE

OUTSTANDING GERMAN SCIENTISTS
BEING BROUGHT TO U.S.

The Secretary of War has approved a project whereby certain understanding German scientists and technicians are being brought to this country to ensure that we take full advantage of those significant developments which are deemed vital to our national security.

Interrogation and examination of documents, equipments and facilities in the aggregate are but one means of exploiting German progress in science and technology. In order that this country may benefit fully from this resource a number of carefully selected scientists and technologists are being brought to the United States on a voluntary basis. These individuals have been chosen from those fields where German progress is of significant importance to us and in which these specialists have played a dominant role.

Throughout their temporary stay in the United States these German scientists and technical experts will be under the supervision of the War Department but will be utilized for appropriate military projects of the Army and Navy.

4:30 P.M.

The German-American scientists Team at White Sands Proving Ground in New Mexico in 1946. The team was also known as "Von Braun Rockets Team".

_____

List of Hitler's and Nazi Germany scientists who worked in Europe and at the Antarctic Base.

Below is a partial list of Hitler's and Nazi Germany scientists from Poland, Austria, Germany and the Antarctica Base who were recruited by Dr. von Braun under the umbrella of Operation Paperclip, the United States government, the military, as well as multi-million Dollars companies in Canada and the United States. The list is by no means complete; it includes a few hundreds instead of thousands. The list includes Nazi scientists, engineers and technicians who worked on advanced weapons systems and related projects, avionics, and propulsion systems, nuclear projects, and later on, worked on similar projects for NASA, the United States Air Force and the United States army.

Nazi German scientists from Europe and the Antarctic Base's blueprints, sketches, illustrations, charts, maps, photos, graphs, and extremely well-documented archives, files and dossiers on various types and classes of anti-gravity flying machines, and experimental flying discs were captured by the United States and Russia after WWII.

- Adolf Grunert
- Adolf Karl Thiel
- Adolf Thiele
- Albert E. Schuler

- Albert Franz Zeiler
- Albert Karl Patin
- Albert Sammeck
- Albrecht Herzog
- Albrecht Hussmann
- Alexander Smakula
- Alfons Fendt
- Alfred H. Henning
- Alfred Kimmel
- Alfred Raimann
- Alfred Renner
- Alfred Schmied
- Allendorf
- Andrae H. Weber
- Anton Beier
- Armin Stelzner
- Arnold Ritter
- Arthur Louis Hugo Rudolph
- August Bringewald
- August Lichte
- August Schulze
- August Wilhelm Quick
- Axel Kolb
- Baron Manfred von Ardenne
- Bernard August Goethert
- Bernhard Duell
- Bernhard Hoeter
- Bernhard Hohmann
- Bernhard Schongs
- Bernhard Tessmann
- Bernhard Wronski
- Bruno Eckert
- Bruno Helm
- Bruno Heusinger
- C. W. Brabender

- Carl Boccius
- Carl Heinz Mandel
- Carl Joachim
- Carl Werner Weihe
- Carl Wilhelm Wagner
- Carlotto Fleischer
- Christoph Schmeizer
- Christoph Soestmeyer
- Constantin Caratheodory
- Decker Stuttgart
- Dieter Grau
- Dieter K. F. Huzel
- Dietrich E. G. F. Singelmann
- Andrik Von Janitzky
- Heinrich Temmle
- Dr. A. Krisch
- Dr. Adolf Baumker
- Dr. Albert (Adolf) Betz
- Dr. Albert Kochendoerfer
- Dr. Alexander Lippisch
- Dr. Alfred Bigalke
- Dr. Alfred Hettech
- Dr. Alfred Kiel
- Dr. Alfred Klemm
- Dr. Alfred Wintergerst
- Dr. Andreas Schilling
- Dr. Anselm
- Dr. Arnold Flammersfeld
- Dr. August Gese
- Dr. B. Schonwald
- Dr. Bachem Konstanz
- Dr. Beerwald
- Dr. Bentele Heinkel-Hirth
- Dr. Bernard Dirksen
- Dr. Borkman

- Dr. Brettschneider
- Dr. Brinkman
- Dr. Bruenig
- Dr. Bruno Wolf Bruckmann
- Dr. Carl Boch
- Dr. Carl Wurster
- Dr. Caspari
- Dr. Cauer
- Dr. Clamann
- Dr. Clemens Muenster
- Dr. Curt Hailer
- Dr. Diedrich Kuchemann
- Dr. E. Emmerich
- Dr. E. Kutzscher
- Dr. Eberhard Gross
- Dr. Egon Heidemann
- Dr. Enno Bussman
- Dr. Erdmann-Jesnitzer
- Dr. Erich Bagge
- Dr. Erich Buchmann
- Dr. Erich Goerner
- Dr. Erich Ruehlemann
- Dr. Erich Scheil
- Dr. Erich Wintergerst
- Dr. Erich Zimmermann
- Dr. Ernst Donath
- Dr. Ernst Franke
- Dr. Ernst Leitz
- Dr. Ernst Nagelstein
- Dr. Ernst O.H. Friedrich
- Dr. Ernst Runge
- Dr. Ernst Ruska
- Dr. Erwin Funfer
- Dr. Eugen J. Sauer
- Dr. Eugen Roth

- Dr. Eugen Sanger
- Dr. Ewald Dickhaeusser
- Dr. F. Heimes
- Dr. Franz Bollenrath
- Dr. Franz Sauerwald
- Dr. Friedrich
- Dr. Friedrich Berkei
- Dr. Friedrich Gottwald
- Dr. Friedrich Hernegger
- Dr. Friedrich Seewald
- Dr. Friedrich Wilhelm Hoffman
- Dr. Fritz Bopp
- Dr. Fritz Brunke
- Dr. Fritz Hartung
- Dr. Fritz Strassmann
- Dr. Fritz Uber
- Dr. Fritz Vilbig
- Dr. Fuchs
- Dr. G. Caspar
- Dr. Geheimrat Herman Meyer
- Dr. Gellendien
- Dr. Georg Cramer
- Dr. Georg E. Messner
- Dr. Georg F. Stetter
- Dr. Georg Hass
- Dr. Georg Korbacher
- Dr. Georg Monia
- Dr. Georg Rickhey
- Dr. Georg Schubert
- Dr. Georg Sichling
- Dr. George Calsow
- Dr. George Gewiese
- Dr. Gerhard Dickel
- Dr. Gerhard Ehlers
- Dr. Gerhard Hassler

- Dr. Gerhard Hyderkampf
- Dr. Gerhard Schmid
- Dr. Gerhard Strauss
- Dr. Gerhard Winfried Braun
- Dr. Gerhardt Schrader
- Dr. Gottfried Guderley
- Dr. Gottfried Max Arnold
- Dr. Guderlein
- Dr. Gustav Bauer
- Dr. Gustav Siebel
- Dr. H. Hilsch
- Dr. Habil Hosemann
- Dr. Habil P. Gorlich
- Dr. Habil W. Bopp
- Dr. Habil Werner Gohlke
- Dr. Hans Bomke
- Dr. Hans E. Hollmann
- Dr. Hans Gorner
- Dr. Hans Gropler
- Dr. Hans Heinrich
- Dr. Hans Hoke
- Dr. Hans Kopfermann
- Dr. Hans Neumann
- Dr. Hans Pabst von Ohein
- Dr. Hans Plendl
- Dr. Hans Plesse
- Dr. Hans Reichardt
- Dr. Hans Rother
- Dr. Hans Sauer
- Dr. Hans Suess
- Dr. Harry Endler
- Dr. Hartig Meyer
- Dr. Heina Schroeder
- Dr. Heinrich Buetefisch
- Dr. Heinrich Cornelius

- Dr. Heinrich Draeger
- Dr. Heinrich Kindler
- Dr. Heinrich Klein
- Dr. Heinrich Rose
- Dr. Heinrich Strombeck
- Dr. Heinz Ewald
- Dr. Heinz Fischer
- Dr. Heinz Pose
- Dr. Heinz Schlicke
- Dr. Helmut Beinert
- Dr. Helmut Heinrich
- Dr. Helmut Sieg
- Dr. Herbert A. Wagner
- Dr. Herbert Altwicker
- Dr. Herbert Boehme
- Dr. Herbert F. Kortum
- Dr. Herbert Koch
- Dr. Herbert Meischeider
- Dr. Herbert Peter Jensen
- Dr. Herbert Ruhlemann
- Dr. Hermann Beuthe
- Dr. Hermann H. Kurzweg
- Dr. Hilpert
- Dr. Hohenner
- Dr. Horhndorf
- Dr. Horst Korsching
- Dr. Horst Rothe
- Dr. Hubert Koch
- Dr. Huebenner
- Dr. Hugo Neubert
- Dr. J. Kaspar
- Dr. Joachim Hansler
- Dr. Johannes Herbert Hoyer
- Dr. Josef Schugt
- Dr. Joseph Dabtscgerm

- Dr. Joseph Schintlmeister
- Dr. Juergen von Klenk
- Dr. K. Doetsch
- Dr. K. Hocker
- Dr. Karl Bammert
- Dr. Karl Berthold
- Dr. Karl Brink
- Dr. Karl Daeves
- Dr. Karl Eisele
- Dr. Karl Erich von Pfaler
- Dr. Karl Fritz
- Dr. Karl Gailer
- Dr. Karl Leistner
- Dr. Karl Ludwig Von Diehl
- Dr. Karl Pohlhausen
- Dr. Karl Rottgardt
- Dr. Karl Steimel
- Dr. Karl Wiegardt
- Dr. Karl Wilfried Fieber
- Dr. Karl Wirtz
- Dr. Klaus Muller
- Dr. Knuth Eckener
- Dr. Kramer
- Dr. Krawinkel
- Dr. Kuehnert
- Dr. Kurt DeBus
- Dr. Kurt Diebner
- Dr. Kurt Hohenemser
- Dr. Kurt Lehovec
- Dr. Kurt Raentsch
- Dr. Kurt Sauerwein
- Dr. Kurt Sennewald
- Dr. Kurt Sitte
- Dr. Lensch
- Dr. Leonard Alberts

- Dr. Leonhard Geiling
- Dr. Leopold Christiansen
- Dr. Ludwig Meyer
- Dr. Ludwig Teichmann
- Dr. Luise Schuetzmeister
- Dr. M. Edelman
- Dr. Martin Eichler
- Dr. Martin Haas
- Dr. Martin Treu
- Dr. Mathias Pier
- Dr. Max Bunzel
- Dr. Max Diem
- Dr. Max Knoll
- Dr. Max Kohler
- Dr. Max Raffel
- Dr. Max Scheurmeyer
- Dr. O. Staiger
- Dr. Oskar Doehler
- Dr. Oskar Vierling
- Dr. Ottmar Stutzer
- Dr. Otto Ambros
- Dr. Otto Dahl
- Dr. Otto Erbacher
- Dr. Otto Hahn
- Dr. Otto Haxel
- Dr. Otto Hecht
- Dr. Otto Heinrich Bock
- Dr. Otto Stierstadt
- Dr. P. Bremmer
- Dr. P. Mallach
- Dr. Paul Hartmann
- Dr. Paul Schmidt
- Dr. Paul Sommer
- Dr. Peter Schlechter
- Dr. Peter Wagner

- Dr. Phil Erich Groth
- Dr. Phil Ernst Heyderbrandt
- Dr. Phil Ernst Lama
- Dr. Phil Georg Klingemann
- Dr. Phil Hans Zirngibl
- Dr. Phil Krefft
- Dr. Phil Waldemar Bielenberg
- Dr. Phillip Von Doepp
- Dr. Prof. Busselmen
- Dr. Prof. Eckhart Vogt
- Dr. Prof. Hans Wieher
- Dr. Prof. Kurt Brand
- Dr. Prof. Von Laue
- Dr. Richard Bieling
- Dr. Richard Braun
- Dr. Richard Kieffer
- Dr. Robert Bosch
- Dr. Robert Saenger
- Dr. Rolf Hermann
- Dr. Rolf Moller
- Dr. Rudolf Edse
- Dr. Rudolf Herman
- Dr. Rudolf Mueller
- Dr. Rudolf Oldenbourg
- Dr. Rudolpf Goethert
- Dr. Rudolph Gebauer
- Dr. Rudolph Koops
- Dr. Rudolph Maria Ammann
- Dr. Siegfried Flugge
- Dr. Sigmund Wintergerst
- Dr. Theo Schmidt
- Dr. Theodor Keilholz
- Dr. Theodor R. W. Gast
- Dr. Titschak
- Dr. Troeger

- Dr. Udo Adelsburger
- Dr. Volker Aschoff
- Dr. Von Bosch
- Dr. Von Holt
- Dr. Von Radinger
- Dr. W. Crone
- Dr. W. Encke
- Dr. W. Frossel
- Dr. W. Knecht
- Dr. W. Koater
- Dr. W. Leikert
- Dr. W. Rein
- Dr. W. Schaefernight
- Dr. W. Soffort
- Dr. Walter Blum
- Dr. Walter Christ
- Dr. Walter Gefken
- Dr. Walter Hermann
- Dr. Walter Rollwagen
- Dr. Walter Wunderlich
- Dr. Walther Werner
- Dr. Werner Czulius
- Dr. Werner Fricke
- Dr. Werner Kluge
- Dr. Werner Kraus
- Dr. Werner Scharwaeghter
- Dr. Wihhelm Runge
- Dr. Wilhelm Buessem
- Dr. Wilhelm Ernstausen
- Dr. Wilhelm Kinner
- Dr. Wilhelm Kleinhans
- Dr. Wilhelm Mueller
- Dr. Wilhelm Oppelt
- Dr. Wilhelm Pleines
- Dr. Wilhelm Stoeckight

- Dr. Wilhelm Walcher
- Dr. Willi A. Kunze
- Dr. Willi Cornelius
- Dr. Willibald Feldmann
- Dr. Willibald Jentschke
- Dr. Willibald Machu
- Dr. Wolfgang Alt
- Dr. Wolfgang Riezler
- Dr. Wolfram Kerris
- Dr. Zschopper
- E. Ernst Vogt
- E. Henning
- Eberhard Fritz Michael Res
- Eberhard Julius Spohn
- Edgar W. Kutzscher
- Edmund Stollenwerk
- Eduard Martin Fischel
- Edward Konstrukteur Heyme
- Emil A. H., Hellebrand
- Emil Johann Walk
- Erhardt Bruenecke
- Erich Bachem
- Erich Bucher
- Erich K. A. Ball
- Erich Kaschig
- Erich Walter Neubert
- Ernest Kramer
- Ernst E. Klaus
- Ernst Geissler
- Ernst Helmut Merk
- Ernst Joseph De Ridder
- Ernst K. H. Huether
- Ernst Rudolf Eckert
- Ernst Sielaff
- Ernst Stuhlinger

- Erwin Kaesemann
- Erwin Neumann
- Erwin Rock
- Eugen Knoernschild
- Eugen Kohlman
- Eugene Neher
- Ferdinand Mirus
- Florian Geineder
- Frank Matossi
- Franz Hollweck
- Franz Huber
- Franz Josef Neugebauer
- Franz Ruf
- Frederick Dhom
- Frederick Doblehoff
- Fredrich Bergius
- Friederich Bielitz
- Friedrich Boettcher
- Friedrich Duerr
- Friedrich Hamburg
- Friedrich Hamman
- Friedrich Otto Adolf Ringleb
- Friedrich Wilhelm Schwarz
- Fritz A. F. Schmidt
- Fritz Hindelang
- Fritz Pflueger
- Fritz Rueff
- Fritz Schwaiger
- Fritz Stamer
- Fritz Vandersee
- Fritz Vollmer
- General Dr. Walter Dornberger
- Georg Klingler
- Georg Knausenberg
- Georg Madelung

- Georg Sutterlin
- Gerd Wilhelm De Beek
- Gerhard Drawe
- Gerhard E Aichinger
- Gerhard Eber
- Gerhard Erle
- Gerhard Heller
- Gerhard Krause
- Gerhard Nehlsen
- Gerhard Schneider
- Gerhardt Hurmann
- Gerold Melkus
- Gertraud Bernhard Duell
- Gottfried Rosenthal
- Guenther Dellmeir
- Guenther Hintze
- Gunter Bohnecke
- Gunther Diedrich
- Gunther Haukohl
- Gustav Hertz
- Gustav Kroll
- H. Bogart
- H. Ziegler
- Hannes Gunther Leuhrsen
- Hans Amtmann
- Hans Brede
- Hans Bussig
- Hans D. Preyer
- Hans Deppe
- Hans Erich Hollman
- Hans Ferdinand Mayer
- Hans Finke
- Hans Fritz Mueller
- Hans Georg Muenzbert
- Hans Gessner

- Hans Gruene
- Hans Guenther Snay
- Hans Henning Hosenthin
- Hans Hermann Maus
- Hans Hueter
- Hans Joachim Oskar Fichtner
- Hans Joachim Rister
- Hans Johann Wiedemann
- Hans Josef Lindenmayer
- Hans Kohlschuetter
- Hans Multhopp
- Hans Paul
- Hans Roskopf
- Hans Rudolf Palagro
- Hans Rudolph Friedrich
- Hans Sallwey
- Hans Sauerland
- Hans Schneider
- Hans Specker
- Hans Ulrich Eckert
- Hans Walter Milde
- Heino Bost
- Heinrich Denstedt
- Heinrich Gruenow
- Heinrich Kuhper
- Heinrich Ramm
- Heinrich Rothe
- Heinrich Wiegand
- Heins Fornoff
- Heintz Gartmann
- Heinz Albert Millinger
- Heinz Beer
- Heinz Dittmar
- Heinz Eugen Schmitt
- Heinz Heithecker

- Heinz Hollmann
- Heinz Leibnitz Maier
- Heinz Ludwig Schnarowski
- Heinz Marcinowski
- Heinz Matt
- Heinz Mueller
- Heinz Pick
- Helmut Hausenblaus
- Helmut Heinrich Schmid
- Helmut Horn
- Helmut Kuhlenkamiff
- Helmut Maetzke
- Helmut Max Arthur Zoike
- Helmut Rudolf Schelp
- Helmut Wilhelm Emil Schlitt
- Helmut Zborowski
- Herbert Bergeler
- Herbert Dobrick
- Herbert Feliya Axter
- Herbert Hans Guendel
- Herbert Jansen
- Herbert Kinder
- Herbert Ludweig
- Herbert Muller
- Herbert Rosin
- Herbert Schwabl
- Herbert Timm
- Herbert Walter Fuhrmann
- Herman E. Lange
- Herman Eutter
- Hermann F. Bedverftid
- Hermann Hagen
- Hermann Joachim Weidner
- Hermann Koehl
- Hermann Kroeger

81

- Hermann Ludewig
- Hermann Mohts
- Hermann Oestrich
- Hermann P. Ehrhardt
- Hermann Symens
- Herr Heep
- Herr Holzapfel
- Herrmann Anscheultz
- Ing. Udo Bolte
- J. B. Goldmann
- Joachim Krause
- Joachim Meyer
- Joachim Wilhelm Muehlner
- Johann Gustav
- Johann Hager
- Johann Klein
- Johannes Finzel
- Johannes Goerth
- Josef Erz
- Josef Hubert
- Josef Krauter
- Josef Martin Michel
- Joseph Bopp
- Joseph Cerny
- Joseph Kuckertz
- Joseph Maria Boehm
- Joseph Wurleszach
- Julius Weindel
- Karl Fickert
- Karl Franz Hager
- Karl Gausman
- Karl Heinrich Gruenwald
- Karl Johann Schmarje
- Karl Koestner
- Karl Ludwig Heimburg

- Karl Neubauer
- Karl Nutz
- Karl Peter
- Karl Petersen
- Karl Ruthammer
- Karl Ryckl
- Karl Sendler
- Karl Voll
- Klaus Eduard Schufelen
- Konrad Dannenberg
- Kraft Ehricke
- Kurt A. Lindner
- Kurt Bredtschneider
- Kurt Daniels
- Kurt Erfurth
- Kurt Hoppmann
- Kurt Jung
- Kurt Kunibert Karlmann Neuhoefer
- Kurt Liebelt
- Kurt Marggraf
- Kurt Paul Erich Patt
- Kurt Strohmeyer
- Lambert Graulich
- Leo Horrec
- Leo. K. Schuesseln
- Leopold Ogthoff
- Leopold Schrader
- Lorenz Schneider
- Lothar Huettuer
- Ludwig Bertele
- Ludwig Karl Vogel
- Ludwig Roth
- Lutz Kleinekuhle
- Magnus Von Braun
- Martha Knoop

- Martin Ruhnke
- Martin Schilling
- Mathias Hickertz
- Max Ernst Nowak
- Max Mayer
- Max Peucker
- Max Sack
- Max Schirmer
- Mosel Wittrich
- Oskar Bauschinger
- Oskar F. Holderer
- Oskar Heil
- Otto August Hoberg
- Otto Buchholz
- Otto Domengen
- Otto Eckert
- Otto Frenzel
- Otto Friedrich Schaper
- Otto Heinrich Hirschler
- Otto Helmuth von Lossnitzer
- Otto K. Eisenhardt
- Otto Knauer
- Otto May
- Otto Muck
- Otto Pabst
- Otto Recknagel
- Otto Schwede
- Otto V. Mueller
- Otto Zimmerman
- Paul Beerbaum
- Paul Duffing
- Paul Friederich
- Paul Herrmann
- Paul Jaensch
- Paul Noack

- Paul Suchy
- Peter Kappus
- Peter Meyer
- Peter Paul Wegener
- Prof. Adolf Busemann
- Prof. Adolf Smekal
- Prof. Blenck
- Prof. Boris Rajewski
- Prof. Curt Otto Schmieder
- Prof. Dr. A. Teichmann
- Prof. Dr. A. Wewerka
- Prof. Dr. Arnold Agatz
- Prof. Dr. Clemens Schaefer
- Prof. Dr. Dietrich Bischer
- Prof. Dr. E. Braun
- Prof. Dr. Edward Grueneisen
- Prof. Dr. Emil Kirchbaum
- Prof. Dr. Erich Siebel
- Prof. Dr. Ernst Von Angerer
- Prof. Dr. Friedrich Harms
- Prof. Dr. Georg Joos
- Prof. Dr. Hans Kuehl
- Prof. Dr. Hans Rau
- Prof. Dr. Hans Rokop
  Prof. Dr. Hans Thoma
- Prof. Dr. Heinrich Hertel
- Prof. Dr. Heinrich Peters
- Prof. Dr. Hrmann Bockhaus
- Prof. Dr. Jonathan Fennick
- Prof. Dr. Joseph Mattauch
- Prof. Dr. Karl Emil Frey
- Prof. Dr. Karl Krauch
- Prof. Dr. Kurt Moeller
- Prof. Dr. Ludwig Bergmann
- Prof. Dr. M. Hansen

- Prof. Dr. Marianus Czerney
- Prof. Dr. Max Franz Berek
- Prof. Dr. Max Seddig
- Prof. Dr. Otto Holfelder
- Prof. Dr. Paul Von Handel
- Prof. Dr. Phil A. Esau
- Prof. Dr. Phil Rudolf Hase
- Prof. Dr. Phil. Erich Moliwo
- Prof. Dr. Phil. Nat. Dieckmann
- Prof. Dr. Phil. Rudolf Brill
- Prof. Dr. Rudolf Geiger
- Prof. Dr. Rudolph Pennorf
- Prof. Dr. Ulrich Dehlinger
- Prof. Dr. W. Tommein
- Prof. Dr. Walter Bauerfield
- Prof. Dr. Walter Georgii
- Prof. Dr. Walter Schottky
- Prof. Dr. Walther Kaufmann
- Prof. Dr. Werner Heinsenberg
- Prof. Dr. Wilhelm Credner
- Prof. Dr. Wilhelm Hanle
- Prof. Eberhard Hopf`
- Prof. Ernst Schmidt
- Prof. Erwin Meyer
- Prof. Fritz Franz Kirchner
- Prof. Fritz Houtermans
- Prof. Georg Barkhausen
- Prof. Gladenbeck
- Prof. Gunther Orther
- Prof. H. Blenk
- Prof. Hans Doetsch
- Prof. Hund
- Prof. Ing. Paul Ruden
- Prof. Karl Friedrich Bonhoeffer
- Prof. Kurt Phillipp

- Prof. Otto Conrad Scherzer
- Prof. Otto Lutz
- Prof. Otto Walchner
- Prof. Otto Zinke
- Prof. Phil Werner Koester
- Prof. R. Fleischmann
- Prof. Rembert Ramsauer
- Prof. Robert Dopel
- Prof. Theodor Rossmann
- Prof. Theodore Buchhold
- Prof. W. Bungardt
- Prof. W. O. Schumann
- Prof. Walter Bothe
- Prof. Walter H. Fichs
- Prof. Werner Kliefeth
- Prof. Werner Schaub
- Prof. Willy Merte
- Prof. Willy Messrschmitt
- Reinhard N. Lahde
- Richard Keiselt
- Richard Lehnert
- Richard Schubert
- Richard Vogt
- Robert Heinrich Karl Paetz
- Robert Lusser
- Robert Lusser
- Rolf Jauernick
- Rolf Krokel
- Rolf Trotz
- Roluf Lucht
- Ross Ropf
- Rudi Beichel
- Rudi Koenig
- Rudolf Franz Maria Homlker
- Rudolf Friederich

- Rudolf Friedrick Hoffman
- Rudolf Hein
- Rudolf Hilsch
- Rudolf Karl Hans Schlidt
- Rudolf Kassner
- Rudolph Opimz
- Siegfried Decher
- Siegfried Erdmann
- Siegfried Guenter
- Siegfried Hasenger
- Siegfried Hoh
- Sighard Hoerner
- Stassfurt-Leopeldshall
- Theo Anton Poppel
- Theodor Bersin
- Theodor Erb
- Theodor Friedrich Sturm
- Theodor Schussler
- Theodor Wilhelm Zobel
- Theodore Sturm
- Ulrich Greuner
- Ulrich Grigull
- W. Hohenner,
- W. Wiebe
- Waldemar Mahn
- Waldemar Moller
- Walter Brisken
- Walter Bunge
- Walter Erdbruegger
- Walter Fritz Wiesemann
- Walter Hans Schwidnetsky
- Walter Horten
- Walter Jacobi
- Walter Klinger
- Walter Kuenzel

- Walter Sauer
- Walter W. B. Burose
- Walther Gustav
- Walther Johannes Riedel
- Werner Barkowski
- Werner Dahm
- Werner Gesche
- Werner Harlin
- Werner Hartenstein
- Werner Hermann
- Werner Koers
- Werner Kurt Gengelbach
- Werner Kurt-Otto Rosinski
- Werner Sieber
- Werner Tiller
- Werner Von Braun
- Werner Von der Nuell
- Wilfried H. Hell
- Wilfried Hell
- Wilhelm Angele
- Wilhelm Bushbeck
- Wilhelm F. H. Knackstedt
- Wilhelm Geyger
- Wilhelm Grunert
- Wilhelm Kollert
- Wilhelm Schaefer
- Wilhelm Schlesinger
- Wilhelm Zumbusch
- Willi Buehring
- Willi Hermann Heybey
- Willi Kaether
- Willi Kretschmer
- Willi Mrazek
- William Prym
- Willie Syring

- Willy Fiedler
- Willy Settmacher
- Wolf Hirth
- Wolfgang Heinemann
- Wolfgang Hermann Steurer
- Wolfgang O. Noeggerath

Hitler's escape of Antarctica.
One of the various accounts of Hitler's escape from Berlin to a base in the Baltic Sea and Antarctica goes like this:
Hanna Reitsch flew Hitler, Eva Braun, Hitler's dog Blondi and General Hermann Fegelein from Berlin to a base in the Baltic Sea, chosen by Admiral Doenitz.
The plan was to land safely on a Nazi base in the Baltic Sea, wait for Hans Kammler who was flying from Poland, and take one of Maria Orsic's Vrils (The Vril was designed by Orsic and built by Dr. W. Otto Shumann's crew in Munich) and fly to Argentina.
This was the original plan.

In fact two airplanes flew from Berlin. One was piloted by Hanna Reitsch, and the other one (As a decoy) by a SS test pilot. Hanna Reitsch landed on the Nazi Baltic Sea base airfield, where two Vrils (Anti-gravity flying discs) were hidden underground, already serviced by engineers from Peenemünde, and ready to transport Hitler and the passengers to Argentina. The two Vrils took off, but one crashed in the Baltic Sea. Hanna Reitsch failed to control the other Vril.

Following her failed attempt to fly the Vril, Hitler changed his mind (he was from the old school and a product of WWI who believed in conventional airplanes and traditional fighters), and ordered Reitsch to land immediately.
Later, Dr. Schumann would explain, "Reitsch could not fly the machine because she did not know how to use the "Head-Band"; apparently an instrument which controls the take off and flight of the airplane. Admiral Doenitz came to the rescue, and suggested that a Messerschmitt Me 262 should be used instead.

90

Upon reconsidering the whole situation, Admiral Karl Doenitz suggested to Hitler that one of his U-Boats should be used, and Hitler agreed.

This version of the story of Hitler's escape was part of:

1-A "Top Secret" United States intelligence agency's dossier on Hitler's escape from Berlin, unrelated to the CIA or the FBI.

2-Notes of Richard Helms, a former Director of Central Intelligence.

3-CIA's files on Adolf Hitler, Escape of Adolf Hitler, Hitler in Argentina, and General Mueller.

4-The Russian secret files on Hitler's escape which was submitted by the NKVD to Moscow.

5-FFL report on Hitler's escape submitted to General Charles de Gaulle.

6-MI5.

7-MI6.

8-SIS.

9-Israel's Irgun Zvai Leumi dossier on Adolf Hitler's escape to Argentina; the Jewish right-wing underground movement in Palestine which was created in 1931, notorious for blowing up King David Hotel in Jerusalem on July 22, 1946.

10-Haganah's files on Hitler and Adolf Eichmann

11-Israe'l Herut files on Hitler and Adolf Eichmann

12-Israel's Mossad files on Hitler, Adolf Eichmann and Nazi war criminals.

13-Account of Dr. W. Otto Shumann.

14-Account of Hanna Reitsch as told to Leni Riefenstahl.

15-Account of Leni Riefenstahl.

16-Account of Lt. Colonel Weimar Norten.

17-Account of Henri Dericourt.

18-Account of Simone Signoret.

19-Account of Jean Gabin.

20-Account of Dr. Richard Miethe.

21-Account of pilot Kurt Tank.

22-Allegedly the account of General Fegelein as reported to Rodolfo Freude.

23-Rodolfo Freude's files on Adolf Hitler.

24-Secretaría de Inteligencia de Estado (SIDE) files on Adolf Hitler.

Anth-Khalka: An Anunnaki term for the creation of the first humans. Composed of two words:
a-An'th, which means race; people.
b-Khalka, which means creation; birth.
From An'th the Arabic word Ounth was derived, which means people, humans, human race. And from Khalka, the Arabic word Khalika was derived, which means creation of the human beings.

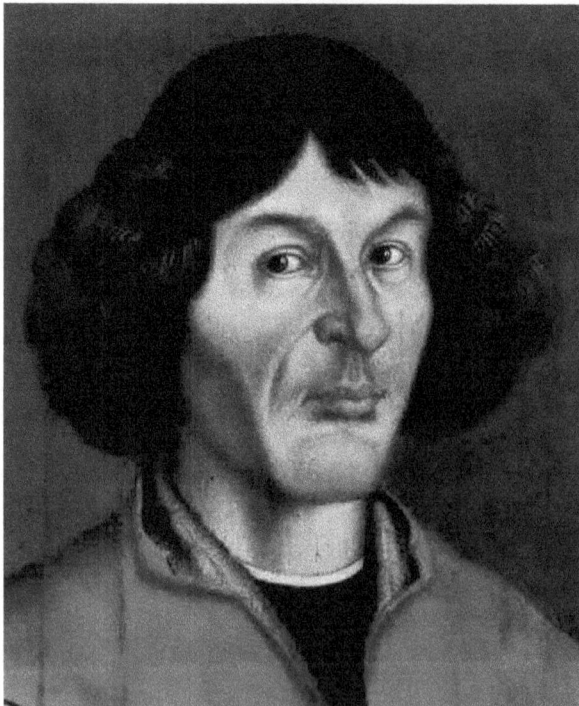

Nikolaus Copernicus (1473-1543): "Life is everywhere in the universe."

**Anthropic principle, Copernicus, and extraterrestrial
life:** Copernicus believed that humanity is not alone in the
universe. Centuries ago, many scientists believed that humanity is
de facto the only intelligence species in the universe. But modern
sciences, cosmology, astronomy and new discoveries of extrasolar
planetary systems in the cosmos proved that life (terrestrial and
extraterrestrial) could exist and/or have existed elsewhere in our
solar system and beyond.

Anti Christ UFOs: A large group of born-again Christians
claimed that UFOs are satanic manifestations od the Devil and
anti-Christ. This belief is widely shared by the believers in the
Rapture. Others are fully persuaded that UFOs are evil and a sign
for apocalyptic events of Armageddon. Some important figures of
organized religions claimed that Satan and the Fallen Angels are
behind UFOs, and the "Alien Deception".
In his article, "Anti-Christ, aliens, and UFOs David Bay, Director
of Old Paths Ministries, wrote, "The drumbeat continues to roll
toward ever higher levels on the theme of UFO's and Aliens
Among Us. This theme has been prevalent in New Age literature
for many years and has developed into an article of religious faith
for many people who have been caught in the lie of the New Age.
However, this theme is now becoming ever more prevalent in the
mainstream media of TV and movies.
Consider the a few of the instances of TV shows and movies which
have carried the alien theme: Close Encounters Of The Third Kind,
Star Trek, E.T., Star Wars Trilogy, TV UFO "documentaries"
abound, including "Unsolved Mysteries".
Let us pause our examination of this UFO/Alien phenomenon for
a few moments as we examine the time frame in which we are
living, and the applicable Biblical framework.
We have already demonstrated that we are living in the Last Days
of time, the time which will see the appearance of Anti-Christ, the
Great Tribulation, and the Second Return of Jesus Christ. And, we
have demonstrated that the hallmark characteristic of the End of
the Age is prophesied to be unparalleled deception.

93

Let us Paul continues, verse 9, "The coming of the lawless one, [the antichrist] is through the activity and working of Satan..." This verse tells us that the source of this End Time delusion will be Satan. Make no mistake about it, Satan's supernatural power will produce the most incredible deception the world will have ever witnessed. This deception will seem so incredible, people's minds will literally be blown away.

At this point, we must remind our listeners that Satan and his angels, also known as demons, are capable of transforming themselves into human and non-human forms so as to deceive people.

As Paul stated so eloquently, "..Satan himself masquerades as an angel of light."

Keep this fact in mind as we study UFO's and Aliens. Without exception, every person claiming an [Alien] contact...had one thing in common. Each had a prior connection to metaphysical activity or cults. Some had been in devil worship, witchcraft, psychic phenomena, New Age, channeling...Those involved in direct contact with UFO aliens already had a connection to the dark side of the supernatural world."

Thus, people today who have thus given themselves over to Satanic activities in some degree are the ones who are being used to deceive people further into believing in UFO's and aliens."

Antigravity fighter disc fleet: Also called the "Lockheed X-224". Some ufologists have claimed that this flying disc is an anti-gravity craft produced jointly by aliens and the United States, and has been regularly used by military astronauts to fly trans-atmospherically to other planets.

Anti gravity RFC-2: In the early sixties, Dr. Winfried Otto Schumann, Professor at the Munich Technical University, told Hanna Reitsch that Hitler escaped on a supersonic-anti gravity "Vril" he built himself using a mind-bending "Metal-Alloy Technology" unknown to scientists.

This craft was called "RFC-2".

The RFC-2 was one of the two small crafts, designed by Maria Orsic, and developed by Dr. Schumann and four engineers.

94

It was an elegant craft with a shiny metallic surface, made from an unknown alloy; it was this kind of alloy the Russians were extremely interested in, because we know that Stalin's NKVD discussed with Dr. Eugene Sänger how such an alloy could be obtained.

Dr. Schumann added, "We built 2 anti-gravity flying machines based upon technical data Maria Orsic received from Aldebaran.

In 1972, Leni Riefenstahl told me: "Hitler and Eva did not die in the bunker in Berlin; they escape with Martin Bormann, two days before the Russians entered the bunker. I know that for sure. I don't know all the details, nobody does.

(My note: Bormann did not escape with Hitler.)

But from what I heard, during his last stand, Hitler received a message from a mysterious woman to get out of Berlin.

The message contained a reference made to a secret airplane capable of flying 6,000 kilometers non-stop (Probably she meant 6,000 miles). People at the bunker did not take the message very seriously.

A second message was delivered to Magda Goebbels. I think it came from Maria Orsic. Magda would not leave her husband.

I am absolutely certain that Hitler, Bormann and Kammler escaped aboard what the Americans call a UFO. The craft made a short stop in Poland and continued its flight to Argentina. People who where very close to Hitler were saying that Hanna Reitsch flew the craft.

Leni continues her story: Two or three years after the war, I heard a new story about Hitler's escape, totally different from the first one, and it goes like this: Hitler, Eva, Bormann and Kammler were taken to a secret location on the Baltic Sea where the Luftwaffe and SS were experimenting with a new kind of airplanes...call them UFOs if you want.

Two special spacecrafts of a bizarre shape were waiting for them. One craft crashed in the Baltic Sea, and the other one managed to fly in an unconventional manner.

Its flight pattern was strange. This very craft took them rapidly to a secret naval base, where they boarded a U-Boat. More SS officers would later join Hitler.

95

They did the same thing...they flew aboard one of the "Vrils" which was stationed in the "Alpenfestung"...they fled the base to South America, and Neuschwabenland without leaving any trace. Two special spacecrafts of a bizarre shape were waiting for them. One craft crashed in the Baltic Sea, and the other one managed to fly in an unconventional manner.

Its flight pattern was strange. This very craft took them rapidly to a secret naval base, where they boarded a U-Boat. More SS officers would later join Hitler. They did the same thing...they flew aboard one of the "Vrils" which was stationed in the "Alpenfestung"...they fled the base to South America, and Neuschwabenland without leaving any trace.

Anti gravity crafts (UFOs), German:
American scientists did meet with Hitler in Argentina in 1956.

A deal was signed or agreed upon between the United States "American Triumvir" and Hitler.

-Was the deal part of the re-emergence of a Fourth Reich? Did Hitler plan on the rebirth of his Aryan race?

-No! The Americans were interested in secret Nazi technology pertaining to space, anti-gravity aircrafts and flying machines (Some have erroneously called them UFOs), some sort of bombs, more destructive than the Atomic Bomb, and so on.

While Hitler's major interest rotated around his own safety, an autonomous Nazi organism free of American and Russian intervention, and above all, an absolute guarantee from the United States that America will not interfere in Hitler's present and future plan to safeguard said "peaceful" organism, which will not cause any threat to the United States.

-Did the United States agree?

-Yes!

-Was the CIA part of the deal?

-No!

-Was the FBI informed? Did Hoover know about the deal?

-No.

-Did Great Britain, France or the Soviet Union know about the Hitler-Triumvir deal?

-No.

-Did the United States Congress know about the deal?
-No.
One of the subjects which was discussed and agreed upon: The renewal of the deal of a Canadian non-fly zone, which was agreed upon in 1952.

Hitler-American scientists meeting after WWII.
After WWII, Dr. Edward Teller, Dr. Wernher von Braun, and Dr. J. Robert Oppenheimer met with Adolf Hitler in 1953 in Argentina. The CIA (created by Truman in 1947; its predecessor was the OSS "Office of Strategic Services") and the NSA (Created by President Truman in 1952; its predecessor was the AFSA "Armed Forces Security Agency which was created on May 20, 1949) never knew about the meeting. Hitler told the triumvir that the New World Order (Germanic New Order) will destroy the United States in a heart beat with Germany's terrifying wonder-weapons (Like Anti-gravity flying machines which Germany could not put to an effective use during the war) should the United States interfere in the GNO's affairs.
Some insiders have claimed that either in Argentina or at the Antarctic German colony, Hitler showed them underground factories of recently developed and manufactured German flying discs and anti gravity crafts of various designs amd shapes such as (To name a few):

Flying discs, triangular anti-gravity aircrafts, tube-shaped crafts, and a huge mothership:
- 1-Die Mutterschiff Einsatzkommando, S1 & S2
- 2-Neuer Bestellugsstrom
- 3-Schwarzer Wind
- 4-Deutsche Tornado-Wut
- 5-Mehrlagige Kuppel
- 6-Die Schwerkraft Aufhebemaschine
- 7-Die Glocke RFZ
- 8-RFC2

Argentina's Juan Perron, who benefited from Nazi Technology,
and opened his doors to Hitler until his death in 1965.

Hitler introduced the triumvir to Juan Peron, who benefited
tremendously from the Nazi's technology. The triumvir also met
with Lt. Colonel Walter Horten and Lt. Colonel Reimar Horten,
inventors of the Horten 229 (H-229) and the lesser known 209 H-
V1. (The H-229 were the half-crescent-shaped, winged crafts
spotted by Ken Arnold, and which were mistakenly called flying
saucers).
And at a later time, Dr. von Braun and Dr. Edward Teller met with
German scientist and Nazi pilot Kurt Tank who was very
important to Juan Peron, because he modernized Argentina' Air
Force.

Under the leadership of Kurt Tank, Argentina produced two highly advanced jet aircrafts, which reached a speed of 1,000 kilometers per hour, the Ta 183 Huckebein, the IA 58 Pucara and the IA 63 Pampa.
Note: The United States and Great Britain tried very hard to recruit Kurt Tank but to no avail.

Kurt Tank

Argentina's Pulqui I displayed at the Argentinean Air Force museum in Buenos Aires. Worth mentioning here that the wing-jet above the Pulqui is Germany's stealth Horten 229, invented by Lt. Colonel Reimar Horten and his brother Walter Horten. Years later, the United States Air Force will copy the German Horten and produced its own version of the stealth wing-jet.

The German Horten flying-wing jet. Below: One of the German Horten first prototypes.

The German flying-wing stealth jet.

The American B2 Spirit. Astonishing resemblance!

The United States Northrop XP-79B flying wing aircraft (version of the German Horten), designed and built in 1945 by Jack Northrop for the US Army. Astonishing resemblance! America's N9-M prototype.

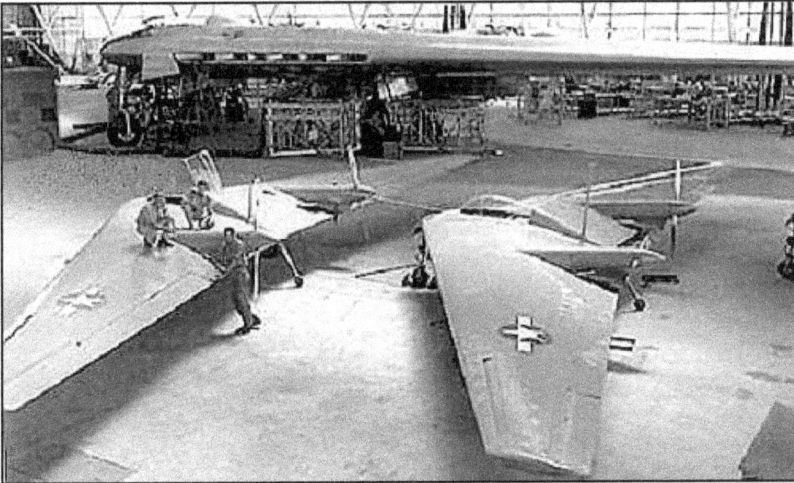

The United States Northrop XP-79B flying wing aircraft (version of the German Horten).

The Russians out of the loop!

The Russians knew what was going on through their agents and spies in Argentina, Brazil, Peru, Portugal, Spain, Sweden and Chile. At one time, they even tried to obtain pertinent information from their "communist" priests-spies inside the Vatican. The Russians did not get the whole picture. They tried again to recruit spies and double agents, as well as new spies from the circle of scientists who worked at Los Alamos.

A former general at the NKVD wrote an extensive report on Hitler-Triumvir's meeting and tried to sell it to Der Spiegel.
The report was either intercepted or allegedly bought by one of America's most powerful families, who in the past financed major enterprises in Germany.

Talking to Hitler.

Dr. J. Robert Oppenheimer did not like what he heard from Hitler and what he saw in Argentina. He was planning on going public. The administration began to watch him very closely.
And Teller enjoyed the show. In 1954, Dr. Oppenheimer lost his top security clearance; it was revoked that year.
The administration discredited him, and he had to face an imminent danger, perhaps death, unless he keeps his mouth shut. This was his life's greatest and most horrifying demise. Many observers link his demise not to his sympathy for communism, but to what he was going to disclose.

The man lost everything, but his life was sparred. He understood that spilling the beans and breaching the oath of secrecy is treason. He faded away.
And all the Glory went to Teller who ironically was a Jew--- go figure!! It was a great opportunity for Teller to get rid of his Los Alamos Boss, Dr. Oppenheimer. He hated him for he was so jealous of his success and fame.
As a matter of fact, in 1954, Teller testified against Oppenheimer in the infamous Oppenheimer's security hearing orchestrated by the administration and the United States Atomic Energy Commission.

Dr. Teller

Dr. J. Robert Oppenheimer testifying before the Joint
Congressional Committee on Atomic Energy, in 1954.

Left: Theodore Hall.

Dr. Edward Teller spread rumors that Oppenheimer was a Russian spy. He was not! The spy was Theodore Hall, a young physicist at Los Alamos.

From the PBS American Experience: "Teller testified very cleverly. And in the years since then, he's denied that he planned it all out in advance, but the record is very clear that he discussed his testimony at least a month before he arrived in Washington, with several people.

Dr. Teller testified that he felt the nation would be more secure if Oppenheimer were not in government. He didn't say he was a security risk. He said, "I would feel personally more secure."

Richard Rhodes stated publicly, "But he (Oppenheimer) was destroyed. And he died.

And that was the end of Robert Oppenheimer.

A really tragic event. The Dreyfus of America, if you will."

What a shameful scam! Rhodes added: "Teller was an outcast, as a result of that testimony. There was a famous incident at Los Alamos soon afterward, where people refused to shake his hand. And he was shaken, and went back to his room, and was extremely upset."

It was so obvious and so bizarre, that von Braun and Teller became "close friends" short after their meeting with Hitler.

History books do not always tell the truth, especially if they are written by the victorious and the powerful.

Intelligent and decent people don't suddenly believe bad rumors and gossip. Idiots and vicious people do, and they rush to give ill and venomous judgments based solely on hearsay and false allegations.

The Internet and many blogers are a perfect example.

The administration remained *à bâtons rompus* in touch with the Germanic New World Order and Adolf Hitler until his death in September 1965.

107

One observer reported that the triumvir learned "alarming and highly significant stuff" from its meeting with the Nazis after WWII, and it was "extremely vital to the national security of the United States, and the future development of extraordinary futuristic weapons programs to be carried out, coordinated and co-accomplished with German scientists." And as history showed us, it did happen.

Working with Nazi scientists and Hitlers' engineers.
It was an <u>absolute necessity</u> for the United States of America to work with Nazi scientists, and cooperate with Hitler's engineers and jet designers in utmost secrecy, in order to develop and improve the United States arsenal, new weapons systems and the United States Air Force capabilities (Stealth and futuristic anti-gravity airplanes, fighters, triangular-shaped crafts, and flying discs.)

German flying disc.

Der Flug des Vril-8 Odin.

One of the United States secret flying discs built upon Nazi Germany's scientific data and blueprints supplied by Hitler's engineers who were recruited by the United States Air Force and worked for NASA, DOE, DOD and USAF. One might think it is a fake photo....so have a look at the photo on the next page...

109

The United States flying disc "Avro Car"; an attempt to copy Nazi Germany flying discs.

United States flying discs on display...finally!!

The United States flying saucers (So to speak) built upon instructions and blueprints provided by Hitler's engineers.

The United States Flying disc Avro Car.

The United States Mach 4.

Anti-gravitational triangular craft: A top secret interstellar craft jointly developed by aliens and the United States at Area 51, and part of the anti-gravity intra-galactic travel research program which includes:
1-The Northrop Grumman B-2 Spirit Stealth Bomber.
2-Lockheed-Martin X-33A.
3-The Aurora.
4-The TR3-Pumpkinseed.
5-The TR-3 B Triangle craft.
Teledyne Ryan Aeronautical XH-75D.
The Shark anti-gravity Helicopter (SC-2).

Levity Disc of John Searl.

Anti-gravity Levity Disc of John Searl: Dr. John Searl is the only man in ufology's history to have built and flown a fully operational anti-gravity craft called "Levity Disc", later called "Inverse-G-Vehicle".

113

Levity Disc of John Searl.

This event was mentioned by the BBC, and written about in numerous newspapers in Great Britain. Some pictures of the craft were published by the Sunday Mirror on November 28, 1971.

John Searl

Antu: Akkadian/Sumerian. Name of the first Sumerian consort of Anu. Their union created the Utukki (The seven evil demons) and the Anunnaki (See Anunnaki). The Utukki were mentioned in the Sumerian and Akkadian "Epic of Creation", and the "Chaldean Genesis".

Anu (Anum): Sumerian/Mesopotamian/Babylonian. Noun.
Anu was the lord of the heavens, the heaven supreme god, and the chief god of the Annunaki.
He is known to the Egyptians as Anu, to the Mesopotamian and Babylonians as An, and to the Akkadians as Anum.
Anu was the eternal sea, the infinite space, and the creator of the gods, including the peoples of Earth. He is Niudimmud's father, and the son of Kishar and Anshar. Antu was his wife.
Their union created many children known as the Anunnaki. His sons were Enlil, Ea, and Ninhursag, also called Ninkhursag.
The Eanna in Uruk was dedicated to him and to his first consort Antu. Their union produced the Anunnaki and the Utukki. His second consort was Inanna (Ishtar). In the Akkadian clay tablets, Anu is depicted as the king of the Igigi.

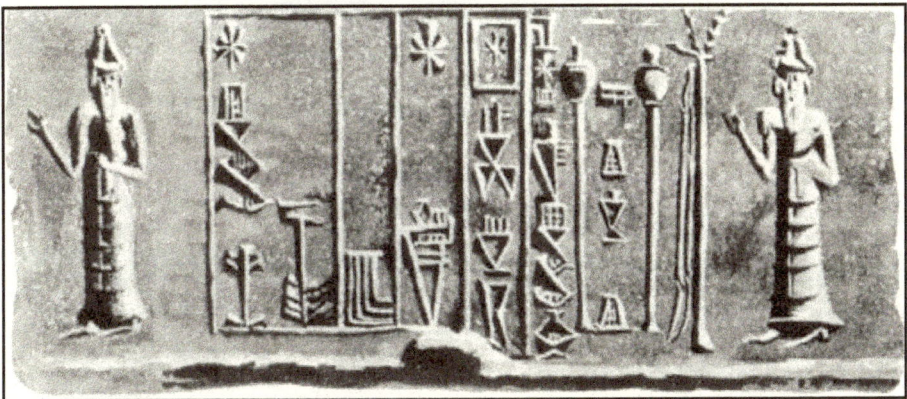

Illustration of Anum (An, Anu) as chief of the Anunnaki.

115

Anum was the creator of the gods, including the peoples of the earth, but over time (3000-2500 B.C.) Anum lost his privileged position to his son Enlil. His main temple was in Uruk, where he was worshipped as the god of that city. Later on, his daughter Inanna became a co-god of Uruk. An mated with the goddesses Ki and Nammu. His union with them gave birth to the gods.

God Anu

"An" or "Anu", the celestial father, and supreme god/Sinhar of
the Anunnaki.

"An", or "Anu", chief god of the Annunaki.
A scene depicting an offering to Anu.

By comparing the size of god Anu to the size of his subject, Anu clearly appears as a giant. In fact, Anu and his Anunnaki's legions were called "Gibborim", "Gababira" (Giants) by the early Hebrews and the Bible's scribes, as well as by the Phoenicians, Hittites, Sumerians and Mesopotamians. The Anunnaki's star is carved on the very top of the slab/cylinder, a reminder/symbol of the celestial origin of the Anunnaki.

All subjects and worshipers before Anu were always depicted as small persons, to reflect the gigantic status of the Anunnaki god, on so many levels, including supreme authority, domination of Earth, and the origin of civilizations on Earth.

118

Subjects bringing dates (Palm dates/fruits) to Anu.

Anunna: Sumerian/Akkadian/Chaldean/Assyrian. Noun.
A collective name for the gods and goddesses of earth and heaven, including the Igigi and the Anunnaki.
Anunna, and Shabbat: The Mesopotamian gods (Anunnaki) created man as an "agricultural slave" to work the fields and to feed them. This is the whole purpose and reason for the existence of the human race on Earth according to the Sumero-Akkadian-Babylonian clay tablets.
In the Babylonian texts, Sebittu, Shapattu or Shabattu meant "resting from toil' also "a ceasing of toil, and resting."

119

Historically, epistemologically and etymologically, the Akkadian word Shapattu referred to what the Akkadians and Sumerians called "the resting of the hearts", or "the resting-day of the hearts." The primordial linguistic-philosophical meaning of *resting of the hearts* could be interpreted as follows: Their hearts are free from grief because finally they (The gods) can rest for ever, since mankind will bear the heavy load of working the fields and feeding them eternally.

The definitions "resting from toil' and "a ceasing of toil, and resting" were cause and effect of the Great Deluge (The Flood).

The Anunnaki sent the flood to destroy mankind because they were noisy, and their clamor prevented the gods from resting (Also sleeping). The flood destroyed mankind in 6 days and 6 nights.

On the 7th day, the Anunnaki rested, because Man no longer existed; finally the gods (Anuna) got their "resting day". Now the Anuna can rest by day, and sleep by night. Sebittu/Shabattu in the Sumero-Akkadian texts (Epic of Gilgamesh, Atrahasis, the Flood, and others) became Shabbat in Hebrew and Judaism.

By using and transforming Sebittu into Shabbat, the Hebrew scribes removed the Anunnaki (Who rested on the 7th day) from the picture, and replaced them with Yahweh for their Saturday (Shabbat, and Sabt in Arabic).

Generally speaking, the Babylonian 6 days of flood which represented destruction and annihilation of the human race, became the 6 days of creation in the Hebrew Bible. And the Anunnaki's "resting on the 7th day" (Older Babylonian texts mentioned the 15th day of the month), became Yahweh's "resting day on the Shabbat."

This transformation was intentionally created by Abraham and his Father Terah from "Ur of the Chakldees", because they did not like the way the Anunnaki established their relation with mankind. It was simply a matter of personal and philosophical opinion.

120

The Hebrew Shabbat once again was transformed to Sunday "Ahad" for the Christians, and called "Yom Al Rab, (meaning the Day of God) and to Friday (Yom Al Joum'ha, meaning the Day of Friday) for the Muslims.

In essence, Sebittu, Shabatt, Ahad, and Joum'ha are one and the very same thing: The day of God.

The Mesopotamian epics made it clear to us that the Anunnaki created mankind to replace the Igigi who complained constantly because of the heavy agricultural work which included working the fields, digging waters' canals, irrigation, planting, harvesting, feeding the gods, and an avalanche of other hard physical works at Nippur, the Anunnaki imposed upon them for many years.

The revolt of the Igigi:

In addition to cultivating and working the fields in ancient Iraq (Babylon, Sumer), Enlil assigned to the Igigi, the hard tasks of digging trenches, canals, and river beds.

And the Igigi kept on doing this hard labor for centuries, until they could not take it anymore. They threw down their tools and went en masse to Ekur, Enlil's citadel at Nippur, to protest this hardship, and to demand immediate relief. When they reached the citadel, Enlil ordered Nusku, his doorkeeper, to keep them out of Ekur.

Nusku asked Enlil:
"Why do you fear your sons?
Call the other gods and
let them help solve this thing."

So Enlil summoned the gods, including Anu and Enki. Together, they rushed to help Enlil, and stood firm on the ramparts of the citadel, and spoke to the furious Igigi:
"Why are you attacking us?

And the Igigi answered:
"The work you have assigned
to us is killing us;
we can no longer bear it.

121

We have stopped digging the trenches
and we are declaring war."

Enki asked the gods for advice, and said to them:
"Why do we blame the Igigi?
Their tasks are too hard.
Goddess Mami is with us.
Let her create beings to serve us
and to do the Igigi's work.
So we can put the yoke of Enlil
on these beings and let
the Igigi return to heaven."

Thus, the Anunnaki decided to create human beings. The Anuna
(The gods) agreed, and asked goddess Mami to create beings to do
the work of the Igigi.
But Mami said:
"It is not wise for me to do all this.
You should choose Enki instead,
because he is wise and
does things right.
But if he prepares the clay
needed to complete the task,
I will create these beings."

Enki replied:
"If we use only clay to create new beings,
they will be like animals,
without intelligence.
Instead, we must slaughter one of the gods,
to make these creatures capable
of bearing Enlil's yoke.
We can mix his flesh and blood
with clay to create a Man."

The Anunnaki seized Geshtu-e, and slaughtered him:
The Anunnaki seized Geshtu-e, the Igigi god of wisdom and
knowledge , and slaughtered him.

As soon as his flesh and blood were mixed with the clay, a Shabbah (Ghost) manifested, and took the shape of a human being.

Mami seized the ghost, and divided him into fourteen pieces, to create seven females and seven males. These creatures were the first prototypes of the human race.

Mami presented her creatures to the Anunnaki, and said:
"I have done everything you have asked.
I have created Man (Men and Women).
And I gave them the faculty of speaking,
so they could talk to each other
and do the job.
Let each Man choose a wife.
And Ishtar will bless them with healthy children,
to fill the whole Earth with generations of servants."

This is why and how Man was created by the Anunnaki at that time in history. Humans were created to do the Igigi's hard labor in the fields, and to feed the Anunnaki. And not to mine gold as erroneously claimed by famous authors in the United States.

Worth mentioning here that Ninmah and Enki genetically created the Lu.Lu; a slave race.

The creation was not totally successful because the Lu.Lu could not reproduce themselves to multiply the population. So Ninmah and Enki decided to create a new race, with the assistance of Ninhursag, Enki's wife.

And the new race was called humans (Bashar). More precisely, a primordial quasi-human form. Lu.Lu was the first specimen of the human race, intentionally created as a laborer or a slave.

Lulu corresponds to Abd, the Anunnaki and Arabic word for a slave. Lulu was created by the Anunnaki goddess Ninhursag. And when men were created, the Anunnaki got their resting day; Shabat in Hebrew.

It is obvious that Hebrew Shabat "The resting Day" is a recast of the Mesopotamian Shabattu, more precisely Sha-pat-tum.

123

In the Akkadian-Sumerian tablets, in the Babylonian List of Words and Vocabulary, as well as in the Babylonian dictionary, both written by the scribes of the era, Shabattu or Sha-pat-tum appeared as follows: " um nukh libbi Sha-Sha-battum."
The Sumerian-Akkadian word "Libbi" for it means heart.
Thus, the proper translation is: "Shabattum, the day of rest of the heart." Literally, it means: The day of rest.
In other words, it means: To cease and/or Ceasing.
Literarily speaking, Shabat in Hebrew means: To cease. In other words, to cease from doing any activity, ceasing from work, or simply put: Ceasing, exactly as the Mesopotamians defined the word in their dictionary.

Anunnaki: Sumerian/Akkadian/Assyrian/Chaldean. Noun.
The Akkadian word Anunnaki is composed of two words:
a-Anunna, which means the entirety of the gods (All the gods and goddesses of Mesopotamia).
b-Ki, which means Earth, and the underworld, the netherworld, and the world of death.
Thus, the correct definition of the word Anunnnaki is: Gods of Earth and/or gods of the underworld.
The Akkadian/Sumerian Anunnaki word is used in a plural form to represent the deities of heaven and Earth, called Anunna in Sumerian and Akkadian.
Later on in history, and in order to differentiate between the Anunnaki and the Igigi, the scribes called the Anunnaki, the gods of Earth (Ki), also gods of the netherworld, and the Igigi, gods of heaven.
This differentiation is very clear in all the Mesopotamian clay tablets, particularly in the Ishtar Descent to the Underworld (Ki), the poem/myth of Gilgamesh, the Enuma Elish, etc...

Other names for the Anunnaki:
The Anunnaki were known to many neighboring countries in the Near East, Middle East, and Anatolia.
And because of the languages' differences, the Anunnaki were called differently.

Babylonia, land of the Anunnaki, at the time it was captured by
the Persians.

For instance:
1- The Habiru (Early Hebrews/Israelites) called them Nephilim,
meaning to fall down to earth, as well as Anakim and Raphaim.
Some passages in the Old Testament refer to them as Elohim.

125

2- In Assyrian-Chaldean, and Syriac-Aramaic, the Anunnaki are called Jabaariyn, meaning the mighty ones.

3- In some Aramaic, Chaldean and Hebrew texts, the Anunnaki are called Gibborim, which means the mighty or majestic ones. Jababira in literary Arabic.

4- The Egyptians called them Neteru.

5- The Greeks called them the Annodoti.

6- In the Book of Enoch, they are called B'nai Elohim (Children of God), the Nephilim, and the "Watchers".

According to some linguists, the word Anunnaki is a loan word from the Sumerian word A.nun "n-a-k", meaning literarily:

a-Semen/descendants of the (Ak) monarch (Nun) and refers to the offspring of the king of heaven An/Anum.

As a group of Akkadian and Sumerian deities, quite often, the Anunnaki were associated with the Anunna, meaning the fifty great gods.

Anuna was written in various forms, such as:

a-A-nun-na,

b-Anu-na,

c-Anuma-ki-ni,

d-Anu-na-ki.

Various attributes or definitions were given to them, such as:

a-Major gods in comparison to the Igigi who were considered minor gods.

b-Those of a royal blood or ancestry.

c-The royal offspring,

d-The great gods of heaven and earth. An means heaven, and ki means earth.

The Annunaki appeared in the Babylonian creation myth/epic, "Enuma Elish".

*** *** ***

126

Anunnaki gods around the Tree of Life.
Nota bene: On two ancient Assyrian obelisks, we read: "Anu sar Igigi va Anunnaki." Translation: " Anu king of Igigi and Anunnaki."
And: "Anu sar El-nuni rabi u Anunnaki." Translation: "Anu king of the great divine chiefs and Anunnaki."

Anunnaki, the Igigi and the creation of Man:
Mankind was not created by one single Sumerian god. More than one Anunnaki participated in the creation of mankind.
And contrary to common belief, the Anunnaki were not the first extraterrestrials and gods to create a human from clay.
Many other deities from different pantheons also created man from clay.

For instance, Khnum "Kneph" (Meaning: To build, to unify in Egyptian) was one of the oldest Egyptian gods, who created mankind from clay on a potter's wheel. Khnum became a variation of Ptah.

Ninhursag/Ninlil/Nama.
Ninhursag, quite often referred to as Ninlil, is shown here as the goddess of irrigation. 18th Century B.C., Mari, Euphrates, Iraq. Courtesy of the Aleppo Museum in Syria.
In several passages from the Akkadian-Sumerian clay tablets, she was also associated with Nanna, who was called the "Creator of Modern Man", and the "Earth Mother Goddess."

There is no reference to one singular creation process or method of the Anunnaki's creation of Man, or a solid certainty to the fact that mankind was created by one single god.
In fact, a multitude of gods and goddesses created different types and categories of human beings, to name a few:
Ninlil:

Ninlil who was also called Aruru, Ninhursag, Ninhursanga, the ruler of the heavens, the Kurnugi, the underworld, and the mother of Nana/Utu experimented with different forms and shapes of early human beings.
Ninlil also created Endiku.

In the Epic of Gilgamesh we read:
"...she created humanity (mankind)...
so many (Abundantly)...
and she pinched clay,
and dropped in the wilderness,
where she fashioned the hero Endiku..."
And in another passage, it was written:
" Endiku my friend whom I loved
turned into clay...
he died...and came back to the clay
that fashioned him..."

Marduk:
Marduk was the son of Ea and husband of Sarpanit, the sun-god, and also the god of war, fire, earth and heaven, and one of the major creators of heroes, gods and humans.
Marduk, Yahweh and the Star Constellation: In a Babylonian myth, called "Enuma Elish", Marduk the god of Babylon, after dismembering "Tiamat", and creating the universe, raised his bow and placed it in the heavens; it became a bow star, more precisely "Star Constellation".
In the Bible, Yahweh did the very same thing; he raised his bow and placed in the heavens. The bow became a rainbow. Chapter 9, Genesis 9:13, "I have set my bow in the clouds, and it shall be a sign of the covenant between me and the earth."

129

Marduk, Baal and Yahweh fightin the dragon:

The Mesopotamian clay tablets told us a story of God Marduk who fought and slaughtered Tiamat the dragon, in order to rule over the world. In the Phoenician-Ugaritic story of "Baal Cycle", the Phoenician god Baal-Hadad fought the Lotan "Tannin" (dragon), the seven headed serpent-dragon of the sea located at a close proximity to Ugarit and Israel.

The Phoenician-Ugaritic dragon story was very well-known to the Hebrews who shared their borders with Phoenicia. In the Jewish Bible, Yahweh fought the sea's dragon Leviathan.

Isaiah 27:1

"In that day Jehovah with his hard
And great and strong sword will punish
leviathan the swift serpent,
And leviathan the crooked serpent,
And he will slay the monster that is in the sea."

Psalm 74:12-14

"Yet God is my King of old,
Working salvation in the midst of the earth.
Thou didst divide the sea by thy strength:
Thou brakest the heads of the sea-monsters in the waters.
Thou brakest the heads of leviathan in pieces;
Thou gavest him to be food to the people
inhabiting the wilderness."

The book of Job describes in detail Yahweh's fight and the fire of the dragon.

Job 41:

"Canst thou draw out leviathan with a fishhook?
Or press down his tongue with a cord?
Canst thou put a rope into his nose?
Or pierce his jaw through with a hook?
His sneezings flash forth light,
And his eyes are like the eyelids of the morning.
Out of his mouth go burning torches,
And sparks of fire leap forth.
Out of his nostrils a smoke goeth,

130

As of a boiling pot and burning rushes.
His breath kindleth coals,
And a flame goeth forth from his mouth."

Unquestionably, the Biblical story of Yahweh fighting the dragon is copied from the "Baal Cycle", an Ugaritic story of god Baa-Hadad who fought against Yam.
The 13th century B.C. myth (Story) of the Phoenician god Baal-Hadad told us that he fought his brother Yam, also called Nahar, to dominate Earth and to rule over the whole world, while the Jewish story was written in 586 B.C.
(Note: Some historians have claimed that the Biblical story was written between 588 and 1200 B.C.)
The Biblical story of God Yahweh fighting Baal-Hadad is simply a reproduction of chapter two of the Ugaritic myth of Yaw (Yahweh) fighting against Baal for the domination of Earth. And the Phoenician dragon mythical story resurfaced once again in the New Testament.

Revelation 13:1
"And he stood upon the sand of the sea.
And I saw a beast coming up out of the sea,
having ten horns, and seven heads,
and on his horns ten diadems,
and upon his heads names of blasphemy."-100 CE.
Many of the early Israelites saw Yahweh as a subordinate to the Phoenician god El. And thus, they equated him with Baal, the Canaanite god they worshiped, and whose attributes were given to Yahweh. Yahweh was depicted as a storm-god who ruled over the waters.
And Baal too, was a storm-god who conquered and dominated the waters, symbolized by a sea serpent and a sea-dragon. The Psalms described Yahweh conquering and subduing the waters by destroying Rab and Leviathan the dragons, exactly as did the Phoenician God Baal who conquered the waters and destroyed the "Tanin", the sea-dragon.
Thus, it is obvious that the Story of Yahweh fighting the dragon originated from the Phoenician story of Baal fighting the dragon.

The triangle, Marduk's symbol appears over the top of a temple, as illustrated on this Kudduru (A boundaries' stone) used by the Sumerians and Akkadians.

Marduk

Marduk, fighting the dragon Tiamat.
Marduk, fighting the dragon Tiamat, and putting an end to her
major influence on the affairs of the universe, the state and Man.
By doing so, Marduk became the absolute and most powerful god
of the Anunnaki, the Igigi, and Babylon.

Marduk chasing and fighting Tiamat.

Eventually, Marduk will slaughter Tiamat, and from parts of her body, he will create the universe, and the early races of humanity, according to the Akkadian-Babylonian tablets.

Akkadian inscriptions of the god-creators of Man, in order of seniority.
A cuneiform Akkadian clay tablet script, 2400-2200 B.C., Sumer, with one single column, listing gods in order of seniority: Enlil, Ninlil, Enki, Nergal, Hendursanga, Inanna-Zabalam, Ninebgal, Inanna, Utu, Nana.

Inanna:
Inanna was the legendary Sumerian goddess who created the first
7 prototypes of mankind.
Many other civilizations worshipped her under different names,
such as Astarte, Istar, Ashtar, Asherah.
Inanna was called Ashtaroot and Ishtar in Phoenician; Ashtoreth
and Ashtaroth in Hebrew; Ashteroth in Canaanite; Atargatis in
Greek.

Inanna on her throne. Circa 2000-1600 B.C., Akkad period.
Nephrite. Cylinder seal. Mesopotamia.

During the early period of the Akkadian reign in Mesopotamia
(c.2334-2154 B.C.), Inanna was associated with Ishtar.
On this Akkadian seal, Inanna (Ishtar) is seated on her throne, and
gestures to two worshippers.
On the left, stands one of her female servants. On the right, a
female attendant pours a libation into a vessel.

137

Inanna

Inanna, the Anunnaki goddess who created Man.

Dumuzi and Inanna bringing gifts to Uruk.

Other names and spellings of Inanna:
- Innin
- Innini
- Ishtar
- Nin-me-sarra
- Ninsianna
- Queen of all the "Me"

- Ninanna
- Nu-ugiganna
- Usunzianna

Inanna appeared in two major Akkadian/Sumerian epics, the "Epic of Gilgamesh," and in the "Cycle of Inanna." She figured prominently in the epic/poem of "Inanna's Descent to the Underworld." This story was written on clay tablets, circa 1750 B.C.

Inanna, standing on a lion, a display of authority.

A 3,000 B.C. Warka vase from Uruk showing a ritual scene of offerings to Inanna, depicted on the very the top of the vase.

Goddess Inanna, known as Ishtar in Akkadian, and Inanna of
Edin, and Nin Edin in Sumerian (Lady of Edin).

Innina:
Name of a great Anunnaki goddess. Innina is the daughter of Sin and Ningal, and sister of Shamash. Her symbol is the eighteen or sixteen-pointed star.
She was worshipped at seven cult centers:

- 1-Arbela
- 2-Ashur
- 3-Babylon
- 4-Calah
- 5-Erech
- 6-Nineveh
- 7-Ur

Innina is also known as Ishtar and the consort of Ashur. According to Ulema Pali, "Innina (Inni-nah) was one of the Anunnaki goddesses who took part in the "fashioning" of Man. And we should not confuse her with Inanna."

Nammu "Namma", "Ninmah":
I. Definition and introduction:
The Sumerian-Anunnaki goddess Nammu/"Namma" and her son Enki created multiple forms of humans, sometimes using clay, and other times using blood of warriors they slaughtered.
In the Sumerian myths, she was the primordial mother goddess, and creator of the gods. She was also called "The pure goddess", and was associated with fresh water.
Nammu is the mother of the Anunnaki god Enki, and the Anunnaki goddess Ereshkigal, the goddess of the Kurnugi (The underworld). The Akkadian/Sumerian texts describe her as "The mother who gave birth to heaven, earth, and the gods of the universe, and the mother of everything."

II. The Divine Feminine:
Heavily inspired by the Anunnaki concept of Nature's Universality, the Mesopotamian scribes depicted and defined her as a goddess without a spouse, the self-procreating womb of the universe.

144

Nammu is a perfect example of the Anunnaki belief in a feminine source of power that created the known universe, including all life-forms. "This Primordial Female Energy" existed long before the universe was conceived and created.

In the Mesopotamian-Anunnaki literature, woman created Man (The first human being), thus sharply contradicting the Jewish, Christian and Muslim scriptures.

III. Nammu, the Anunnaki goddess who first thought of creating Man:

Nammu is the Anunnaki goddess who gave Enki the idea of creating humankind to replace the Igigi, who worked the fields.

Enki begins to think about the creation process, and how to use the clay and water of the abyss, to create human beings.

He told Nammu to bring Anunnaki womb-goddesses to mix the clay and to call upon Anunnaki fashioners (Term used to refer to Anunnaki goddesses who designed the body of the first Man) to thicken it, so she could mold the wet clay into the shape of a human body.

Then, he instructed her to bring the limbs to life, in the image of the gods. She will give birth to the embryo of mankind without using the sperm of a male.

The new being shall be called Adamah. And a creature was created. Then, the gods and goddesses decided to have a feast to celebrate their new creation, and Enki and Ninmah began to drink beer and got drunk.

Consequently, the being they created was a deformed creature. And Ninmah continued to fashion handicapped people.

Her creations were:

    a-A weak person who was unable to control his urine,

    b-A barren woman,

    c-A being without organs, etc.

Finally she realized that she was unable to create a perfect Man. She throws down the clay in despair. Then Enki decided to create a man by himself, but he failed, for the creature he fashioned died as soon as he was born.

145

A drawing from a cylinder seal of King Gudea of Lagash, circa 2100 B.C. shows Ningishzida as a human with serpent-dragon heads, and as a four-legged beast with horns and wings.

Enki as Ea:
I. Introduction:
Ea killed Kingu, the demon son of Tiamat, and used his blood to create mankind. Ea created Zaltu to complement goddess Ishtar. Ea was one of the earliest Anunnaki who gave instruction to Anunnaki goddesses, including Aruru, on how to create the first prototypes of Man, to replace the Igigi who were assigned hard physical labor in the fields and gardens of Sumer.

II. Definition:
Ea is the name of the son of Nammu and An. Sometimes he is mentioned as the son of Anshar. Enki was the Sumerian god of water. He was also known as Ea in Babylonian mythology.

Ea "Enki" stepping on dry land, a gesture symbolizing his
supreme authority over Earth.
The dry-land as depicted in this cylinder seal, refers also to
ramparts protecting the cities of his kingdom. From the ramparts
emerge a stream of fishes, symbol of all life-forms in the seas.
Thus, his authority extends to dry lands and seas of the Earth.

He lived underground in huge lakes and in deep waters called
Apsu. Enki is also called En.uru, which means lord reed-sheaf.
He had several epithets, such as:
1-"Enki bël nagbï. Bël derived from Bëlum, which means lord.
Nagbi derived from Nagbum, which means a spring.

147

Anunnaki God Ea accompanied by two deities in the form of a
scorpion and a dragon.
A slab from Tell Asmar in Iraq, depicting the Anunnaki God Ea,
accompanied by two deities in the form of a scorpion and a
dragon. The scorpion represented wisdom and determination,
while the dragon represented authority and the primordial
female aspect of the Creation.

2-"Sar apsi", means king or lord of the Apsu. Sar (pronounced
Shar) derived from Sarum (pronounced Sharum), which means
king and/or a prince).
3-"Ea Mummu bani kali." Bani means a builder (Bani in Arabic
also means a builder). Mummu means a genius. The translation
is: "Ea, the genius who built everything."
4-"Enki Bel nemeqi", meaning Enki a master-craftsman.

Enki's name can also be interpreted as "Lord of the Earth," because En means a lord, and Ki means Earth. But Ki means also hell, the underworld, the world of no return.

It is derived from the Akkadian/Sumerian word Kurnugi, which means the underworld, the empire of death. Thus, Enki becomes the lord of the underworld. Enki lived in Eridu, in his temple É-abzu (Apsû).

A drawing from Gudea's cylinder seal showing King Gudea of Lagash, Ningishzida and the seated god Enki.

II. Enki's plan for creating the human race:
Synopsis of the translation of the original Sumerian texts; Nintu
and Enki plan the creation of the human race (I: 178-220); Enki,
rather than Anu, is speaking at this time. In these versions, Enki
reveals his plan for creating the human race.

Note: God Enki is speaking when the story continues:
"While Nintu the birth-goddess is here,
let the birth-goddess create the offspring...
let man carry (Hold) the labor-basket of the gods."

Enki and Nintu called the goddess and said to her:
"You are the goddess of creation,
The creator of man.
Create now the Lullu-man,
let him bear the yoke.
let man carry the labor-basket of the gods."

And Nintu said to the Anuna (The great gods):
"It is not my job to do this.
He is the one who purifies all;
let him give me the clay,
and I will do it."

Enki said to the great gods:
"At the beginning of the new moon,
On the seventh day,
I will set up a purifying bath.
And let them kill on the gods.
Let purify the gods by immersion.
With his blood and flesh
Nintu will mix the clay.
And let man and God in the clay
be inseparable till the end of time.
Let there be life from the flesh of god.
Let there be life (spirit)."
The purifying bath was set up,
And We-ila was slaughtered in the assembly.

With his blood and flesh Nintu mixed the clay.
And from the flesh of the god there was life.
She (Nintu) announced he is alive.
After she finished mixing the clay,
She called the Anunnaki, the great gods.
The Igigi cast their spittle on the clay.
And Mami said to the great gods:
"You ordered me to do this, and
I have completed it.
You killed a god and I have removed you
From this heavy labor...
The gods heard her speech,
They were pleased and kissed her feet,
And the great gods said:
In the past we called you Mami.
But from now on, you will be called
The mistress of all the gods.
Again and again she chanted an incantation.
When she completed her incantation,
She nipped off fourteen pieces of clay.
She placed seven pieces on the right,
And seven pieces on the left,
Between the pieces she placed the brick.
She patterned the flour and laid down the brick,
And the goddess of creation said:
I completed my creation,
My hands have done it.
Let the brick be laid down for nine days.

Note: The Assyrian tablets revealed that fourteen birth goddesses fashioned the clay to create seven males and seven females and align together in pairs.

*** *** ***

Geshtu-e: The slaughtered Igigi god and the creation of the "First Man", from the first Babylonian version:

151

I. Definition/introduction: Geshtu-e is the Akkadian/Sumerian name of the Igigi god whose blood and intelligence were used by the Anunnaki Mami to create the first man. In the beginning, before men were created, the Anunnaki, the had to till the land and water it to grow their food. And this was hard and extremely demanding labor. Enlil summoned the Igigi, and asked them to do the job.

Ekur

II. The Igigi's revolt: In addition to cultivating and working the fields in ancient Iraq (Babylon, Sumer), Enlil assigned to the Igigi, the hard tasks of digging trenches, canals, and river beds.

And the Igigi kept on doing this hard labor for centuries, until they could not take it anymore. They threw down their tools and went en masse to Ekur, Enlil's citadel at Nippur, to protest this hardship, and to demand immediate relief. When they reached the citadel, Enlil ordered Nusku, his doorkeeper, to keep them out of Ekur.

Nusku asked Enlil:
"Why do you fear your sons?
Call the other gods and let them help solve this thing."

So Enlil summoned the gods, including Anu and Enki. Together, they rushed to help Enlil, and stood firm on the ramparts of the citadel, and spoke to the furious Igigi:
"Why are you attacking us?
And the Igigi answered:
The work you have assigned to us is killing us;
we can no longer bear it.
We have stopped digging the trenches
and we are declaring war.
Enki asked the gods for advice, and said to them:
Why do we blame the Igigi?
Their tasks are too hard.
Goddess Mami is with us.
Let her create beings to serve us
and to do the Igigi's work.
So we can put the yoke of Enlil on these beings
and let the Igigi return to heaven.

III. The Anunnaki decided to create human beings:
The gods agreed, and asked goddess Mami to create beings to do the work of the Igigi.
But Mami said:
"It is not wise for me to do all this.
You should choose Enki instead,
because he is wise and does things right.
But if he prepares the clay needed to complete the task,
I will create these beings."

153

Enki replied:
"If we use only clay to create new beings,
they will be like animals, without intelligence.
Instead, we must slaughter one of the gods,
to make these creatures capable of bearing Enlil's yoke.
We can mix his flesh and blood
with the clay to create a Man."

IV. The Anunnaki seized Geshtu-e, and slaughtered him:
The Anunnaki seized Geshtu-e, the Igigi god of wisdom and knowledge , and slaughtered him. As soon as his flesh and blood were mixed with the clay, a Shabbah (Ghost) manifested, and took the shape of a human being.
Mami seized the ghost, and divided him into fourteen pieces, to create seven females and seven males. These creatures were the first prototypes of the human race.

V. Mami presented her creatures to the Anunnaki, and said:
"I have done everything you have asked.
I have created Man (Men and Women).
And I gave them the faculty of speaking,
so they could talk to each other
and do the job.
Let each Man choose a wife.
And Ishtar will bless them
with healthy children,
to fill the whole Earth
with generations of servants."

Note: This is why and how Man was created by the Anunnaki at that time in history. Humans were created to do the Igigi's hard labor in the fields, and to feed the Anunnaki. And not to mine gold as erroneously claimed by famous authors in the West!!

*** *** ***

Imma-shar:
I. Definition: Name of one of the goddesses who participated in the creation of Man.

154

She is also called a "Fashioner", because she helped in designing and fashioning the looks of the first genetically created man. In the Sumerian Epic section "Birth of Man", we read the following:

Note: After instructing his mother to get more goddesses to help in the creation of humans, the god Enki produces a fetus, limbless and lifeless. Shortly thereafter, god Enki instructs the goddesses on how to create the first humans.

II. The Akkadian text on the creation:
Once you are done with mixing the
the Apsu's clay,
and placed the limbs over it
Imma-en and Imma-Shar will
Enlarge the fetus.

Enki then gives additional instruction to goddess Ninmah, who is the mother goddess, and to eight Anunnaki goddesses.

He said:
O mother, once, you have finished molding the being,
let Ninmah unite the chair of birth,
without using male semen, and then,
you give life to mankind.
Without the sperm of males
she will create their offspring,
and give life to the embryo of mankind.
And once Nammu had increased the size of its shoulders,
she will punch a hole in the head to place a mouth.
Note: The following line is damaged.
and afterward, she will wrap the body in an amnion.

Note: The tablets tell us that Enki and Ninmah got drunk, and consequently, they created crippled beings; they were both physically and mentally deformed. Enki then decided to create a creature on his own. The Epic tells us that this creature (Quasi-Human) is terribly deformed.

III. Excerpt from the Akkadian text:
Ninmah says:
The man, you fashioned (Created)
is neither a living being (A man),
nor a dead being (A man),

The Akkadian clay tablets tell us that the creation of the first Man required the participation of at least twelve Anunnaki goddesses. They had to mix up the "fathering clay" of the Apsu, which is the underground fresh water.

The clay the Anunnaki goddesses have used, had very particular properties that produced life, once joined with a woman's womb. The clay was later placed over the fetus and fashioned into the form of man. Once done, the Anunnaki goddesses added limbs and a mouth. To complete the genetic creation of Man, Ninmah placed the clay into her womb.

Note: This is one version of the creation of the first Man, for the Akkadian tablets offered different stories of how the Anunnaki genetically created several prototypes of mankind.

Anunnaki's symbols: The winged disk.

The Anunnaki's winged disk (Their symbol) over the tree of life surrounded by two guardians, as seen on the next page.

Because of the supernatural power attributed to the Anunnaki's wings, many ancient civilizations in the Middle and Near East, including the Egyptians and the Persians adopted these wings as their royal symbol.

The Anunnaki-Egyptian wing, as adopted by Rameses III. Luxor, Egypt.

Isis wing.

Faravahar, the Persian royal wing.

A "Winged Disk", a symbol for the Anunnaki, as it appeared on numerous Babylonian clay tablets.

Anunnaki's symbol in an Egyptian/Roman burial chamber.

The Anunnaki's wing appears in a secret ritual invocation in a Roman/Egyptian burial chamber, Kom el-Shugafa, Alexandria, Egypt.

Ashur as King of Babylon dressed into an Anunnaki motif.

The Symbol of Ashur depicting the three manifestations of Elohim or Gods. Ashurai kings were servants of God. They were the first king-priests of ancient times.

Ashur's symbols.
Left: Feather robed archers.
Right: The winged disk on a Kudduru (Boundary stones).

Anunnaki's symbol in Egypt:

The Anunnaki wing becomes the sun disk of Egyptian God Ra.

The Sumerian chariot and Anunnaki's symbol.

The Sumerian chariot was one of the major military innovations in history. However, several Egyptians and Hittites plaques and slabs have revealed that the invention and use of the chariot in the battlefields should be credited to the Hyksos, who invaded and ruled Egypt for centuries.

Other historical records of the era demonstrated that the early Hyksos (Offspring of the remnants of the Anunnaki in Anatolia) were the first to use a horse and a chariot in a battlefield.

Notice the Anunnaki-Babylonian symbol above the charioteer: The Anunnaki's wing.

Each time, this symbol appears on an inscription or a slab, it reveals the royal status of the personage depicted on the stele.

The Anunnaki Wing symbol was carved in a prominent place on Sumerian-Babylonian slabs, cylinder seals and tablets, for two reasons:

- **1-**To explain and confirm the presence (Leadership) of a Babylonian king, because the wing was in itself a royal emblem.
- **2-**To protect the king and his troops, because the Sumerian-Babylonian believed that the Anunnaki's wing was a "Divine Shield", and a sign of a heavenly authority on Earth.

Serpent God:

The serpent was an Anunnaki-Phoenician-Ugaritic-Arwadian symbol used by the "Milkart Circle", the "Serpent Brotherhood", and by the Anunnaki-Ulema Society, as a logo for science and discovery.

Later on, it was adapted by many neighboring civilizations as a divinity symbol, and as a sign for the celestial guardians of monarchs' life, and protectors of their tombs.

The Egyptians accorded a place of honor to serpents in their religion, myths, tradition, science and literature.

It was not always the sign of the devil or demonic temptation as erroneously depicted in the Judeo-Christian-Muslim traditions.

Egyptian king of the gods, Amen Ra, being protected by the twin guardian serpents, while standing at the main entrance of the "Door of Mysteries".

The concept of the "Egyptian Door" was conceived/shaped after the Anunnaki's Ba'ab.

Similarity resides in the "Personal spiritual liberation", and the final destination of the king (Sinhar in Ana'kh) in the sphere of stars.

Sumerian serpent gods.

Amen Ra

Anunnaki's hidden symbols.

Note from the editor: Unusual find on the Internet.
The following illustrations were sent to Maximillien de Lafayette by one of his readers, asking him to verify the veracity of captions under the photos as appeared on the Internet. "I will not comment on what it was posted on the Internet. Instead, I will provide my personal comments and interpretations. And for the record, I am herewith reproducing the illustrations as received." See explanations on the next page.

Symbol #1: It is a cross.

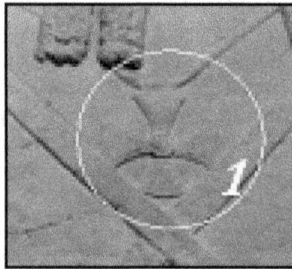

The very same cross used by Les Templiers "The Templars" (The early design used by the Knights Templar in Jerusalem, Malta, and Cyprus, see below.)

But there is more!
Do you know what this cross means? It means and represents the ultimate energy in the known universe.
In ancient times, it meant the "Philosopher Stone", the "Elixir of Life" (The Anunnaki Haf-nah), the source of longevity (ORME); the formula the Templars and alchemists used to transmute metal into gold. In modern times, it means: Nuclear Energy.
Atomic radiation! Here is the logo/sign:

Symbol #2: The Anunnaki's Mushroom. Ulema de Lafayette has discussed this topic in his books.

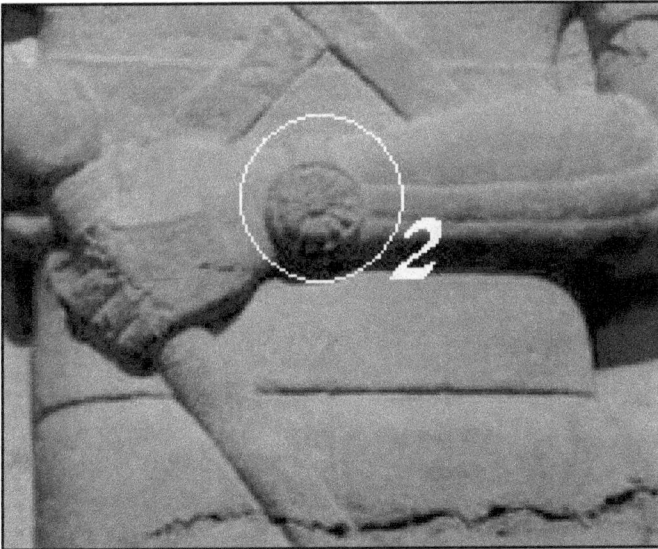

The "Rosette" as referred to by art historians is in fact a cross surrounded by leafs. In fact, it is a cross composed of a small circle in the center, surrounded by four branches. This was the Anunnaki's symbol of Haf-Nah and Amrit. See next page.

169

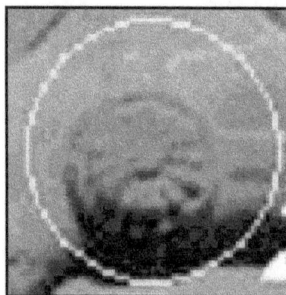

Symbol #3: An Annunaki Sinhar pushing one particular point (a button) on the perimeter of a "Cadre"; the bubble of the universe, or the cocoon of the extraterrestrial dimension, to open the Ba'ab (The Anunnaki's gateway of a stargate)

Anunnakifalak "Dounia": Akkadian/Anak'h/Ulema/Arabic.
The universe of the Anunnaki.
Excerpt for a Kira'at (Reading) by Ulema: As far as humans are concerned, there are two Anunnaki's worlds:
1-Sama,
2-Falak.

According to the Ulema, the first world is the Sama. The second world is the Falak, or Dounia: Falak "Dounia" is not a physical world. No living human beings as physical creatures live in this second world.

"You have to remember that physical objects including human beings cannot enter a non-physical world, unless their molecules are reduced to a lower level of vibrations..." said Ulema Al Bakri.

"Thus, Falak "Dounia" is not a world where human beings could live with their physical bodies. Falak "Dounia" is the world of the human mind. The human mind was created by the Anunnaki. The human mind can manifest itself as the Double of a physical body..." explained Ulema Raja Shinkar.

Falak consists of seven different "Woujoud", meaning existences. Three of these Woujoud already exist in a physical-nonphysical sphere of illusion, called "Kha-Da'h".

Planet earth is one of these three existences. But these three existences do not count as meaningful dimensions. This is why we start counting with the Fourth dimension as the first sphere of Falak.

a-The first Woujoud is known to us as the Fourth dimension, and it is called "Nafis-Ra".

b-The second Woujoud is known to us as the Fifth dimension, and it is called "Fik'r-Ra".

c-The third Woujoud is known to us as the Sixth dimension, and it is called "Kadosh-Ra" or "Koudous-Ra".

d-The fourth Woujoud is known to us as the Seventh dimension, and it is called "Khalek-Ra".

In other words, the Falak is the world of human beings who continue to live through their mind.

171

Extraterrestrials of a very high vibrational state could share this sphere with the purified mind of humans (The deceased ones).

Falak starts as soon as we die. It is neither outside nor inside our solar system, and no light years separate humans from any dimension or state of existence in Falak.

Some Bashar (Human beings) have already reached different vibrational levels and spheres in Falak "Dounia".

Anunnaki-Sama "Shama":

Akkadian/Anak'h/Ulemite/Arabic/Aramaic/Syriac.

One of the other dimensions of the Anunnaki.

Excerpt for a Kira'at by Ulema: As far as humans are concerned, there are two Anunnaki's worlds: "Sama" and "Falak".

The first world is the Sama: It exists while humans are still alive on planet earth.

Sama is the extraterrestrial world, where the Anunnaki and other extraterrestrial races live. Sama existed in the universe billions of years before planet earth and the human race were created. Sama is a physical world. Its atmospheric properties vary from one planet to another planet, and from one star to another star.

For instance, Ashtari has quasi-similar earth's atmosphere, however the air is denser, the climate is heavier, the days are longer, and it has four celestial objects orbiting it.

Although humans could live on Ashtari certain surgical operations are needed to allow the human body to adapt to the new atmospheric conditions and environment on Ashtari.

So, the physical world of the Anunnaki would allow humans to continue to live outside planet earth, and inhabit Ashtari. You could call Sama the bodily world of humans, because humans can travel to Sama and live on Sama as physical creatures.

Sometimes we refer to Sama as "Maddi", meaning the physical dimension outside planet earth. And Maddi has living conditions almost similar to those on planet earth. Maddi has weather, trees, lakes, plains, mountains, cities, streets, etc.

In other words, the Sama is the world of the living human beings, and extraterrestrials. It starts outside our solar system; billions of light years separate planet earth from Sama. Bashar or Naas (Human beings) have not reached Sama yet.

172

But extraterrestrials have reached planet earth some 500,000 years ago (More or less). Some extraterrestrial races are still on planet earth, and have offspring and descendants living among us.

Anunnaki-Shabka: Anak'h/Akkadian/Sumerian/Phoenician/ Arabic. Expression. The name of a spatial web or net.
It is composed of Anunnaki+Shabka (Net).
Net should be understood as a matrix.
Excerpt for a Kira'at (Reading) by Ulema: The Anunnaki Matrix is many things indeed. It is larger than anything the human mind could possibly imagine. It contains the entire past, present and future of multiple dimensions and civilizations, including planet Earth, and the human races. Ulema Rushdi Anafawi Takiyeddine said: "There are three matrices known to mankind:
1-The Anunnaki's Matrix;
2-The Ulema's Matrix;
3-The Humans' Matrix."

Ulema Raji Khandar said: "Each matrix has its own dimensions, contents, and scope. However, the Anunnaki's matrix includes the Ulema's matrix, the Ulema's matrix includes the humans' matrix, and the humans' matrix includes exclusively our habitat on planet Earth."
This matrix is extremely complicated, because it is written in codes, symbols, geometrical forms, chemical formulas, theorems, and in all the languages that have existed, still exist, and will be invented in the future after 2022, according to the Ulema.
In other words, it is a cosmic library, archives, and depository of all the knowledge and events of 5 billions years, the estimated date of the beginning of the universe.
According to the Ulema, and Al-Munawarin, the Anunnaki's matrix' scientific data/registry contain all the explanations of the creation of our universe (Solar system, all stars, planets and galaxies known to us.) Included in the data/registry are detailed descriptions and explanations of:
1-Primordial bio-engineering of terrestrial life (Elements, nature, animals, and humans.)

2-Building blocks of life, and how they acted like cells to produce life on earth.

3-DNA's fifth unknown element.

Ulema AlKhabir said: "So far, scientists on earth have discovered 4 elements in our DNA: Cytosine, Thymine, Adenine and Guanine. In the Anunnaki's Matrix, there is a fifth element called "I-Bra.Ah", meaning transcending time and space in the Ana'kh language."

The Ulema coined it "Niktat Alkhou-Lood", and it means verbatim: The point of the beginning of immortality. In other words, the fifth element is responsible for an extraordinary longevity of mankind on earth, and/or its immortality.

It is very possible said an Ulema that after 2022, humans will learn about the secret of immortality, but will never be able to decode the composition and sequences of the fifth element.

"It would be a catastrophe for humanity and for the future of planet earth, if humans succeed in decoding the data contained in the fifth element..." said Ulema Benadar Gupta.

Many Ulema are not seriously worried, because with the arrival of the Anunnaki in 2022, the existence of human life and its continuity will be in the hands of the Anunnaki, according to Ulema Gupta.

4-RNA and Life Evolution: In addition to the DNA, the Anunnaki's matrix gives detailed information about the RNA, which is a ribonucleic acid, a close cousin of deoxyribonucleic acid or DNA.

RNA is a polymer of ribonucleoside-phosphates. Its backbone is comprised of alternating ribose and phosphate groups.

Ribose is a five carbon sugar that is found in a puranose, or five-membered ring, form in RNA.

The phosphate groups link consecutive ribose groups and each bears one negative charge. Each monomer also has a nitrogenous base for a side chain.

The Anunnaki's matrix includes a fifth base in the RNA chain, and it is called in Ana'kh "Ta-Tawur-Ankh".

The Ulema interpreted it as the "Evolution of life on earth". The Anunnaki explained how this fifth base created the primordial molecules that duplicated themselves and consequently started the life evolution cycles on planet Earth.

Do the Anunnaki speak or understand our languages?
Languages on Earth:
All our spoken languages derived directly from extraterrestrial languages. And all terrestrial languages derived from the Phoenician Alphabet.

Many of the Phoenician linguists and early creators of their Alphabet borrowed numerous words and expressions from the higher class of the Anunnaki. Ancient Phoenician texts and poems, recorded on tablets found in Tyre, Sidon, Ugarit, Amrit, and the Island of Arwad included reference to symbols and words taken from the written language of the upper class of the Anunnaki.

The first genetically created race could not speak, and the concept of language was completely unknown to humans. Thousands of years later, the Anunnaki taught the new race of humans how to speak, read, and write. Members of an early Anunnaki expedition to Phoenicia taught the Phoenicians how to create their language, and revealed to them the secret powerful names and attributes of Baalshalimroot. They instructed them not to use these words for ill purposes. Particularly, the word "Baalazamhour-Il" is never to be said, spelled, or written. Later on in history, the Hebrews religiously observed this instruction, and pronouncing the word of name of God became forbidden.

The language of the Anunnaki was taught to the early Phoenicians who lived in the ancient cities of Tyre, Sidon, Byblos, Afka and Batroun. Phoenicia borrowed her Alphabet from the Anunnaki.

The 7 powerful names and attributes of the Anunnaki's grand leader were given to the early Phoenicians in a ritual ceremony in Tyre.

Yes, extraterrestrials are capable of speaking and understanding many languages, including our own. They assimilate and "compute" words and sentences with mathematical formulas and numerical values.

Some extraterrestrials have limited vocal chords capabilities, but they can very quickly acquire additional vocal faculties by rewinding sounds and vibes. Contrary to what many contactees and others said, extraterrestrials from higher dimensions do not talk like computerized machines.

They have their own language but also they can absorb and assimilate all the languages on earth in a blink of an eye via the reception and emission of a "spatial memory."

At first, the voice of an alien from a higher dimension sounds like an old record that was played at the wrong speed – fast, squeaky, scratching. Then the sound adjusts itself, and the voice becomes a normal human voice.

A very pleasant human voice.

Many of the Anunnaki's letters cannot be pronounced by Westerners because of the limitation of their vocal chords.

Anunnaki's language used by Americans:
The American top military scientists who work in secret military bases and aliens' laboratories on earth have an extraterrestrial lexicon, and use it constantly. In that lexicon, or dictionary, you will find variations of Phoenician and Sumerian symbols.

Some particular letters represent maritime and celestial symbols and measurements.

The fact that the Americans are still using this extraterrestrial language should be enough to convince you that the US deals with extraterrestrials, and Zeta Reticuli descendants, live among us, otherwise why would anyone learn a language that cannot be used to communicate with people who speak it and write it?

On some of the manifestos of military parts used in anti-gravity secret laboratories underground in the United States, several letters were borrowed from the "Enuma Elish" of Sumeria and regularly appeared on the top right corner of each document.

In the eighties, those Sumerian numbers were replaced by an Americanized version. Military personnel at other American military bases in Mexico, Australia and underwater in the Pacific do not use an extraterrestrial lexicon.

The original language of the Anunnaki is still intact and is currently being used by top American scientists and researchers who work in secret American-Aliens military bases in the United States and Mexico.

In 1947, the first attempt was made by American linguists, who previously worked at the OSS (Precursor to the CIA), to decipher it. They tried to compare it with the Sumerian, Hebrew, Armenian and Phoenician Alphabet, languages which are directly derived from the Anunnaki's written language. The problem they faced and could not resolve were the geometrical symbols included in the written Anunnaki's texts. But in 1956, they cracked down the puzzle. Those mathematical figures hold great secrets regarding an alien advanced technology used for peaceful and constructive purposes.

The American military intelligence and what's left from Dr. Fermi's group at Los Alamos wanted to use this alien technology for military purposes.

The Anunnaki have two kinds or styles of languages; one is spoken and the other one is written. The spoken language is the easiest one to learn, and it is used by the Anunnaki's population.

The written one is exclusively used in books and consists of twenty-six letters. Seven of these letters represent the planets that surround their planet.

Feelings and reactions: Do Anunnaki feel and react like us? Yes! The Anunnaki Express Emotions.

There is a major misconception about the Anunnaki's emotions and the nature of their feelings. Avalanches of erroneous theses were written about their cruelty, ferocious reptilian character, and particularly about abducting humans. Among the most considerate extraterrestrial races are:

1-The Lyrans;
2-The Nordics;
3-The Anunnaki.

Unfortunately, misinformed writers wrote chapters upon chapters describing how the Anunnaki and their (Nizlat) remnants on earth control our mind and disrupt the order in our societies, because they have a malicious agenda.

177

The truth is, the Anunnaki do not interfere in human affairs. They have left earth centuries ago. Those who are abducting humans are the "Grays". The Anunnaki express their feelings just like we do. However, they do not shed tears, nor succumb to emotional crises.

Their "sentimentality" is controlled by a "Conduit" directly linked to a community-collective-awareness.

This means, that their emotions are regulated – but not controlled – by an "intellect" channel. This channel is constantly balanced scientifically.

The female Anunnaki are more affectionate than their male counterparts. For instance, at the Anunnaki Academy of Learning, male Anunnaki have developed the space-time travel, remote viewing and "cosmic projection" courses.

Per contra, the female Anunnaki have developed arts and "social communication" study programs.

This comparison is self-explanatory. And if we go back in history, we discover that the genetically created men by male Anunnaki looked like robots and machines, while the final "product" of the early modern men as created by the female Annunaki had more appealing physical attributes, and more developed sense for aesthetics and artistic creativity.

Do The Anunnaki react and feel like us? They do not react like humans, but they do express emotions and feelings. Because their society is matriarchal in essence, the Anunnaki are deeply influenced by the female nature and element which translate into compassion, and devotion for their families.

Many of the Anunnaki look like us. They share with humans many physical properties, and to a certain degree, a "partial" DNA! The Igigi did co-exist with the Anunnaki, and shared some traits with them, but they were totally dissimilar in their physical shape, and had different intentions as far as the human race was concerned.

The Igigi are 245 million years older than the Anunnaki.
The lower class of the Anunnaki are the Nephilim, although many historians call them sometimes Anakim or Elohim.

The higher class of the Anunnaki is ruled by Baalshalimroot, and his followers or subjects are called the "Shtaroout-Hxall Ain", meaning the inhabitants of the house of knowledge, or "those who see clearly."

Ain: The word "Ain" was later adopted by the early inhabitants of the Arab Peninsula. "Ain" in Arabic means "eye".
In the secret teachings of Sufism, visions of Al Hallaj, and of the greatest poetess of Sufism, Rabiha' Al Adawi Yah, known also as "Ha Chi katou Al Houbb Al Ilahi" (The mistress of the divine love), and in the banned book *Shams Al Maa'Ref Al Kubrah* (Book of the Sun of the Great Knowledge), the word "eye" meant the ultimate knowledge, or wisdom from above.
"Above" clearly indicates the heavens. Later on, it was used to symbolize the justice of God or "God watching over us." And much later in history, several societies and cultures adopted the "eye" as an institutional symbol and caused it to appear on many temples' pillars, bank notes, money bills, and religious texts.

Anunnakifalak Dounia: Term for the multiple universe of the Anunnaki. Falka-du'nia in Ana'kh and Ulemite. Falak-Dounia in Arabic.

Anunnaki's stargate: Also called Ba'ab, Bab, Babu, Babi, etc. in several ancient and dead languages. A term for an entrance and an exit to multiple worlds, stars, planets, and galaxies.
See Ba'abs (Stargates).

Anunnaki's Chronology: Anunnaki and Their Time on Earth
1,250.000 years ago:
The Anunnaki are not the oldest extraterrestrial race, because we don't know at all how many different extraterrestrial races and inhabitable planets and stars exist in the known and unknown universe.
However, we do know from the Book of Ramadosh (Rama-Dosh) and other obscure but reliable sources, that the Anunnaki are the early galactic race (From outer space) to land on planets Mars and

179

Earth, and to established colonies in different regions of our planet, encompassing the lands of Central Africa, Madagascar, Australia, a region of Europe, with a strong concentration in ancient Phoenicia and Iraq. T
he early edition of the book of Ramadosh (Rama-Dosh) also refers to the Anunnaki's primordial colonies and their spatial stations on Mars, before their arrival to planet Earth.

In one of the Fousool (Chapters) of the Book, the scribes explained the reason and motives of the Anunnaki's expedition to Earth. In a sharp contrast with a common belief, the Anunnaki did not land on Earth to mine gold.

Note: The extraterrestrial bio-aquatic research center theory surfaced in United States government secret files shared with NSA and NASA. In these files, references were made to currently existing non-terrestrial facilities, habitats, bases, laboratories, and "strange" communities under water on planet Earth; all in the hands of an extraterrestrial race.

The Anunnaki along with the Lyrans (Lyrians, also Lyriyan) and Narim (Nordic extraterrestrial race) are the only humanoid race/extraterrestrial race to resemble modern human beings to a certain degree.

1,250.000 years ago, the Anunnaki Edi-Majla was established.

450,000-460,000 B.C.:

Anunnaki's first landing in Phoenicia:

The Anunnaki landed in the fields and on the shores of what we call today Lebanon.

The word "Lebanon" derived from the Akkadian and Assyrian words Libnana and Lubanu, and means"white". Egyptians began to use it in the third Millennium before Christ, and references were made to Lebanon in manifestos and letters pertaining to cedar wood shipments from Lebanese cities to Egypt.

The Greeks called the lands "Phoenicia".

It is derived from the Greek word "Phoenix", meaning purple-red. And purple red was the dye (Ourjouwan) extracted by the Phoenicians from the mollusk shell-fish.

It was used to color linens and fabrics. Purple-red was the royal color of the Anakh (Anunnaki.) The Anunnaki began to build their first colonies on Earth. They established the cities of Saydoon, Tyrahk, Kadmosh, Adonakh, Ilayshlim, Markadash.

a-Saydoon became Sidon and Saida;

b-Tyrakh became Tyre and Sour;

c-The Phoenician "Kadmos" is named after Kadmosh;

d-The Phoenician god "Adon" is named after Adonakh. Adon or Adoon became Adoni and Adonai in Hebrew.

e-Ilasyshlim gave birth to the words: El, Al, Eli, Elohim, Ilahi, Illah, Allah (In Anakh, Sumerian, Phoenician, Aramaic, Hebrew and Arabic.

f-Markadash became Byblos (named by the Greeks) and Jbeil (named by the Arabs.) Jbeil is possibly the oldest city in the world. Archaeologists have uncovered houses of farmers, peasants and fishermen in Jbeil going back to 7,000 B.C.

Byblos (Jbeil), today.

181

Some of the homes currently occupied by the inhabitants of the region are built on the top of historical foundations and ruins dating back to the days of the early Phoenicians, remnants of the Anunnaki. Archeologists found one-room huts with crushed limestone floors and basins, and a slab of god El known to the Phoenicians as Baal and El.

The Sea Castle at Sidon.

It was built and used by the Crusaders for multiple purposes known to historians. But the esoteric history of Sidon told us, that many of the Crusaders fortresses and castles have served as secret centers for Near Eastern esoterica, the occult and the study of Sihr.
Sidon was one of the earliest colonies of the Anunnaki on Earth.

The ancient castle and harbor of Sidon.

Book Ilmu Al Donia , and the Book of Ramadosh told us that it was around the harbor of Sidon, that the early Anunnaki's expeditions to Earth retrieved the green and red algae much needed in their genetic and scientific experiments.

Sidon

View of Sidon during the Islamic Occupation and what was left from Phoenicia, the land of the Anunnaki.

The Reconstruction of the Upper Square of Sidon, From the Prince of Wales's Urban Design Task Force.

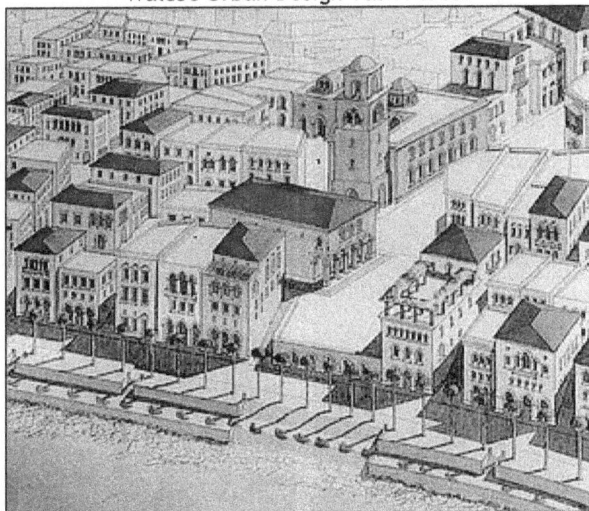

The reconstruction of the Lower Square and Corniche of Sidon.

Sidon (Saida), today.

Tyre during the Islamic Occupation of Lebanon (Ancient Phoenicia).

Tyre as Sour, some 60 years ago. Once upon a time, Tyre was one of the earliest Anunnaki's colonies on Earth.

449,000 B.C.: Under the leadership of Enki, the Anunnaki landed on Earth. The Anunnaki established their first colonies on the lands of Phoenicia, Syria and Iraq. But their first cities and housing facilities were erected near Baalbeck, followed by Eridu. The Anunnaki used a sort of laser beams (anti-gravity tools) to lift and transport enormous stones exceeding 1,500 tones each to build their first labs, landing and launching pads and to strengthen their strongholds.

Their operations extended to regions neighboring Iran, Jordan and Israel. Years later, they concentrated their operations in Sumer and Africa, where they built enormous cities. However, during their first expedition, the Anunnaki did not relinquish the colonies they established in Phoenicia (Baalbeck and Tyre). The first Anunnaki's expedition included a multitude of scientists, land and space topographers, irrigation experts, engineers, architects, metallurgists, mineralogists, and military men.

A swastika sign on one of the Jupiter Temple's column in Baalbeck, linking the builders of the temple/early inhabitants of Baalbeck to the esoteric masters of Tibet, and the extraterrestrial gods of India (Hindu and Buddhism).

188

The six legendary columns of Baalbeck.
One of the columns of Baalbeck.

One of the columns of Baalbeck.

The Trilithon of Baalbeck.

The base of the Temple of Jupiter is called the Trilithon, and it is constructed of three 1200-tonne limestone megalithic stones. Legend has it, that the temple was constructed by a fleet of giants sent by Nimrod. An ancient Arab fable tells us that the Afrit of King Solomon built the temple. Others have claimed that the city of Baalbeck was constructed by the Anunnaki.

Baalbeck was major occult and a healing center visited by many kings and emperors. Attracted by its beauty and supernatural properties, the Roman emperor Augustus made Baalbeck a Roman colony and a major oracles shrine. In fact, the Roman emperor Trajan consulted a celebrated oracle in Baalbeck.

Unfortunately, Baalbeck was totally sacked and decimated by the Muslim Arabs in 748 A.D. In 1,400 A.D., Turkish conqueror Tamerlane pillaged and destroyed the city, and several Roman-Phoenician-Anunnaki temples and altars. In 1,759 A.D., a major earthquake decimated the remaining ruins and almost all what was left from the Anunnaki-Phoenician monuments.

There is one place on earth, the Ulema consider as the ultimate "terminal" of the Anunnaki; a sort of a Ba'ab from which a person enters or exits a physical dimension. And that place is Baalbeck.

Thousands of years ago, and long before the Sumerians, Akkadiand and Assyrians established their kingdom in Iraq, and interacted with the Anunnaki, and many many centuries before the human race in any region of the world learned about God or Gods, the Anunnaki landed in Baalbeck, and revealed to its inhabitants many secrets, including teleportation, psychic healings, and the divine nature of the supreme beings (Gods, creators). Baalbeck served them as a landing and a launching post. It still exists today.

446,000-445,000 B.C.:
This marks the Anunnaki's second massive landing on Earth.

440.000-430.000 B.C.:
More Anunnaki landed on Earth. In the Phoenician waters, the Anunnaki searched for aquatic bacteria such as fungi much needed for the development of certain organs of the Homo Sapiens.

415,000-416,000 B.C.:
With the arrival of Anu and Enlil on Earth, a major part of the Anunnaki's expansion operations shifted to the Central African continent. Enlil was in command of the whole enterprise, and became powerful on Earth ruling the Anunnaki living in the Near East, Middle East and occasionally in Africa.

Enlil relinquished his authority in Africa to Enki, and planned on returning to Ashtari. A mutiny exploded in the Sumer lands headed by the grandson of Alalu.

400,000 B.C.:
The Anunnaki established seven large settlements in the southern region of Mesopotamia that included:
a-Enormous metallurgical center in Shuruppak.
b-Several space launching and landing pads controlled by centralized center in Sippar.
c-A space travel command center in Nippur and Baalbeck.

380,000 B.C.:
A war waged by the Enlilites devastated the region. This was a perfect timing for Alalu's grandson to re-seize power, especially that the Igigi gave him full military support. These were turbulent days for the Anunnaki. Marduk's allies, the Igigi, ruled vast estates and irrigated lands in Phoenicia (Modern Lebanon) and Sumer. Nabu, Marduk's son, summoned these Igigi communities to Marduk's city, Babylon, to build a launch tower from which Marduk could challenge the Enlilites.

350,000 B.C.:
The mining of Earth's natural resources (Not gold!) operations of the Anunnaki expanded on a very large scale. More manpower was needed.
The Anunnaki requested the help of their leaders both on Earth and Nibiru, but remained in vain. So the Igigi revolted against them. One option was left for the Anunnaki: They asked Enki to create a race to do the heavy physical work of the Igigi.
Anunnaki called this new race "The workers", while the Igigi called them "the slave race".
With genetic manipulations, they created the Lu.Lu slave race. This race was created by combining Igigi DNA/blood and genes from the Homo-Habilis, who were the most advanced primates living on earth at that time.

Revolt of the Igigi:

193

In addition to cultivating and working the fields in ancient Iraq (Babylon, Sumer), Enlil assigned to the Igigi, the hard tasks of digging trenches, canals, and river beds.
And the Igigi kept on doing this hard labor for centuries, until they could not take it anymore.
They threw down their tools and went en masse to Ekur, Enlil's citadel at Nippur, to protest this hardship, and to demand immediate relief. When they reached the citadel, Enlil ordered Nusku, his doorkeeper, to keep them out of Ekur.
Nusku asked Enlil:
"Why do you fear your sons?
Call the other gods and let them help solve this thing."
So Enlil summoned the gods, including Anu and Enki. Together, they rushed to help Enlil, and stood firm on the ramparts of the citadel, and spoke to the furious Igigi:
"Why are you attacking us?
And the Igigi answered:
"The work you have assigned to us is killing us;
we can no longer bear it."
We have stopped digging the trenches
and we are declaring war."
Enki asked the gods for advice, and said to them:
"Why do we blame the Igigi?
Their tasks are too hard.
Goddess Mami is with us.
Let her create beings to serve us
and to do the Igigi's work.
So we can put the yoke of Enlil on these beings
and let the Igigi return to heaven."

The Anunnaki decided to create human beings:
The gods agreed, and asked goddess Mami to create beings to do the work of the Igigi.
But Mami said:
"It is not wise for me to do all this.
You should choose Enki instead,
because he is wise and does things right.
But if he prepares the clay needed to complete the task,
I will create these beings."

Enki replied:
"If we use only clay to create new beings,
they will be like animals, without intelligence.
Instead, we must slaughter one of the gods,
to make these creatures capable of bearing Enlil's yoke.
We can mix his flesh and blood
with the clay to create a Man."

The Anunnaki seized Geshtu-e, and slaughtered him:
The Anunnaki seized Geshtu-e, the Igigi god of wisdom and knowledge , and slaughtered him.
As soon as his flesh and blood were mixed with the clay, a Shabbah (Ghost) manifested, and took the shape of a human being.
Mami seized the ghost, and divided him into fourteen pieces, to create seven females and seven males. These creatures were the first prototypes of the human race.

Mami presented her creatures to the Anunnaki, and said:
"I have done everything you have asked.
I have created Man (Men and Women).
And I gave them the faculty of speaking,
so they could talk to each other
and do the job.
Let each Man choose a wife.
And Ishtar will bless them
with healthy children,
to fill the whole Earth
with generations of servants."

Note: This is why and how Man was created by the Anunnaki at that time in history. Humans were created to do the Igigi's hard labor in the fields, and to feed the Anunnaki. And not to mine gold as erroneously claimed by famous authors in the West!! The idea of "Anunnaki mining for gold on Earth" is naïve.
Some passages from the Babylonian epics told us that Ninmah and Enki genetically created the Lu.Lu; a slave race. The creation was not totally successful because the Lu.Lu could not reproduce themselves to multiply the population. Ninmah and Enki decided to create a new race, with the assistance of Ninhursag, Enki's wife.

195

And the new race was called humans. More precisely, a primordial quasi-human form. Lu.Lu was the first specimen of the human race, intentionally created as a laborer or a slave.

272,000 B.C.:
Enlil expelled Adam and Eve from the Garden of Eden (Janat Adan, Edin). Enki interfered to "upgrade" the DNA of Adam and Eve, so both could reproduce.
The Anunnaki genetic composition of Abel, and how he fits in the Anunnaki-Bible equation:
In order to explain the genetic composition of Abel, an Ulema suggested that we should ask ourselves what kind of relation Eve and her children had with God and the Anunnaki. There is a vast literature about Eve, and lots of contradictory accounts about her true nature, her origin, her DNA, and above all, her relation to the Anunnaki, the Gods, and the Judeo-Christian-Muslim God.
Eve appeared in the Sumerian texts, in Phoenicians epics, in the Bible, in the Quran, in the Gnostics books, and in the Ulema's manuscripts.

Eve story in the Bible is the less credible one. In some passages of the Sumerian texts, En.Ki as a king, a god and a creator, created Eve.
However, according to other Sumerian texts and Anunnaki's mythology, it is not absolutely clear if En.Ki was the original and sole creator of Eve, because many other Sumerian deities participated in the creation of mankind, such as Angel Gabriel known as Gb'r, Inanna, to name a few.
Humans who were genetically created by the Anunnaki were produced from and by a mixture of the DNA of an Anunnaki, usually a god or a goddess, and an earthy element.
This element was described as either clay or specie of a primitive human being.
The intervention of an Anunnaki god was a prerequisite.

Thousands of years later, the Bible told us that Eve too received a divine help in the creation of her first two sons; they were fathered by the Lord not by Adam.

This could and would astonish the Christians. Eve conceived Cain and Abel with the help of God. Only her third son Seth was the result of her union with Adam. And Seth came to life in Adam's likeness. So how did Cain and Abel look like?
The Bible does not provide an answer.

- From Genesis: 4:1 "...and she bore Cain saying: I have gotten a man with the help of the Lord. And again, she bore his brother Abel..."
- From Genesis 5:3: "When Adam had lived a hundred and thirty years, he became the father of a son in his own likeness, after his image, and named him Seth."

The Gnostics books shed a bright light on this situation; Cain was created by the Anunnaki god Enki, and a woman called KaVa, (Also Havvah and Hawwa) which is the original name of Eve in the ancient texts written thousands of years before the Bible was written and assembled.
This is the official version of the Gnostics. This means that Cain is not 100% human. Cain's blood is ¾ or ½ Anunnaki.
The other two sons of Eve, Abel called "Hevel", and Seth called "Sata-Na-il" were less than ½ genetically Anunnaki, because they were the offspring of KaVa (Eve) and Ata.Bba (Original name of Adam).
Cain was superior to his brother Abel at so many levels, because he was the offspring of an Anunnaki.
Abel was inferior to Cain, because he was the offspring of an earthy element.
The superiority of Cain was documented in the Bible, because the Bible (Old and New Testaments) clearly stated that Cain "rose far above Abel"!
Thus, the Ulema, conclude that:
1-Eve and Adam were not from the same race. Genetically, they were different.
2- The offspring people (First human race) of Eve were the result of a breeding by Gods.
3-The children of Abel and Cain were genetically modified to fit the scenario of the Anunnaki.

197

4-The creation of the human race happened earlier, much earlier than the date suggested by Jewish, Christian and Muslim scriptures.

5-All human races came from the primordial female element: Eve.

200,000-195,000 B.C.:

In Africa, the human races working for the Anunnaki near Ethiopia's Omo River began to enjoy a limited autonomy. These races were considered by the Anunnaki to be the precursors of the most advanced human races on Earth.

Note: The existence of these human races was certified by modern science.

According to the National Gographic, "the human fossils found 38 years ago in Africa are 65,000 years older than previously thought, a new study says—pushing the dawn of "modern" humans back 35,000 years.

New dating techniques indicate that the fossils are 195,000 years old. The two skulls and some bones were first uncovered on opposite sides of Ethiopia's Omo River in 1,967 by a team led by Richard Leakey.

The fossils, dubbed Omo I and Omo II, were dated at the time as being about 130,000 years old. But even then the researchers themselves questioned the accuracy of the dating technique.

The new findings, published in the February 17 issue of the journal *Nature,* establish Omo I and II as the oldest known fossils of modern humans.

The prior record holders were fossils from Herto, Ethiopia, which dated the emergence of modern humans in Africa to about 160,000 years ago.

"The new dating confirms the place of the Omo fossils as landmark finds in unraveling our origins," said Chris Stringer, director of the Human Origins Group at the Natural History Museum in London.

The 195,000-year-old date coincides with findings from genetic studies on modern human populations.

Such studies can be extrapolated to determine when the earliest modern humans lived. The findings also add credibility to the widely accepted "Out of Africa" theory of human origins which holds that modern humans (later versions of Homo Sapiens) first appeared in Africa and then spread out to colonize the rest of the world. Life on planet Earth began to regress during a new glacial period."

160,000 B.C.:
First recorded court testimony in history; Enoch testified against the "Sons of God" who have committed a major sin, and broke the laws of the Anunnaki by having sexual relationships with the "Daughters of Man" (Daughters of Humans).

125,000-100,000 B.C.:
This is the last interglacial period, and the weather was as warm as the present climate. The human races were not yet fully integrated into the Anunnaki's society, because they were not yet considered a genetically complete race.

During those years, the Anunnaki began to create the final format (mentally and physically) of humans. The final format reached its last phase around 65,000-60,000 years ago.

At that time in history, prosperous Anunnaki cities were already established in Sumeria, (Ur), Syria (Ugarit, Island of Arwad, Amrit), part of Jordan (Batra), Baalbeck, Jbeil, Tyre and Sidon in Phoenicia (Modern Lebanon today). Also during that period, the Anunnaki created the early human women and were called "Women of the Light"; they were the early female-forms on Earth. Contrary to all beliefs, including what Judaism, Christianity and Islam teach us, Eve was not created from the rib of Adam. Men were created from an early female form that was "fertilized" by the leaders and the elite of the Anunnaki.

They lived in quarantined cities, and had both sons and daughters fathered by the Anunnaki. Early humans who lived during that era called the quarantined city of these women "The City of Mirage", and "The City of Beautiful Illusion," since the most attractive women from earth lived there. And the quasi-humans who were made out of earth were not allowed to interact with these women. Thousands of years later, the inhabitants of what is today the Arab Peninsula and the lands bordering Persia, the United Arab Emirates, and India, called these women "The Women of Light", and those who were allowed to "mix with them" were called "The Sons of Light".

199

From this early human race, all humans came to life. The Judeo-Christian God had nothing to do with the creation of the human race. In other words, the God we know, revere, and fear today did not create us.

Even the word or term "God" did not exist in the early stages of the existence of the human race on earth.

The goddess Lilith with bird features in the center, has been identified with Lilith. 2000-1600 B.C. Isin-Larsa-Old Babylonian period. Hematite. Cylinder seal. Mesopotamia.

A note on the "Women of Light":

- 1. The "Women of Light" were the early female-form on Earth.
- 2. Lilith and Eve were from the "Women of Light" group, created by the Anunnaki.
- 3. Their untraceable genealogical line, which is neither human, nor from the act of the Judeo-Christian-Muslim God, puzzled the ancient scribes, Biblical scholars and historians of all eras.

- It is an untraceable genealogical line, because both Lilith and Eve don't have a father.
- 4. And if they did, their father, and their mother wouldn't be of human origin.
- 5. Eve was not created from the rib of Adam.
- 6. Different racial categories of men were created from an early female form that was "fertilized" by the leaders and the elite of the Anunnaki.
- 7. They lived in quarantined cities, and had both sons and daughters fathered by the Anunnaki.
- 8. Some Anunnaki dwellings were in Ur, Amrit, Ougarit, Baalbeck, Batroon, Petra (Batra), Tyre and Sidon.
- 9. Early humans who lived during that era called the quarantined city of these women "The City of Mirage", and "The City of Beautiful Illusion," since the most attractive women from Earth lived there.
- 10. The early inhabitants of the Arab Peninsula called these women Houriyaat".
- 11. Originally, the word "Houriyaat" is an Ana'kh (Anunnaki language) word. Later on, it was added to the Arabic language, and to the Afarit (Djinns) terminology.
- 12. The quasi-humans who were made out of Tourab (earth, mud, dirt, soil), were not allowed to interact with these women.
- 13. Thousands of years later, the inhabitants of what is today the Arab Peninsula and the lands bordering Persia, the United Arab Emirates, and India, called these women "B'nat Al-Nour", meaning "The Women of Light."
- 14. A mild variation of the Anunnaki word B'nat became a Hebrew and an Arabic word "Banat", which means daughters. And the Anunnaki word Nour, which means light, became Menora in Hebrew, and Noor in Arabic.
- 15. Those who were allowed to "mix" with the Women of Light were called "The Sons of Light".
- 16. From this early human race, all humans came to life. God had nothing to do with the creation of human beings.

- 17. In other words, the God we know, revere, and fear today did not create you.
- 18. Even the word or term "God" did not exist in the early stages of the existence of the Women of Light, and the primordial human race on Earth.
- 19. Instead the words or terms "Gods" or "Heavenly Masters" were used.
- 20. And thousands of years later, those terms were changed to:

a- "Giants,"
b- "Gibborim,"
c- "Jababira,"
d- "Raphaim,"
e- "Bene-Ha Elohim,"
f- "Elohim,"
g- "Nephilim,"
h- "Anakim,"
i- "Fallen Angels,"
j- "Neteru,"
k- "Anuki,"
l- "Anunnaki,"
m- "Ana'kh,"
n- You name it...

75,000 B.C.:
A new Ice Age begins. Handful of remnants of the quasi human races previously created by the Igigi roamed the Earth, later to be totally extinguished. In other parts of the world, variations of the Cro-Magnon man survived for a short period.

70,000 B.C.:
1-Enki genetically created Noah; he was born with a sparkling white skin, and large black eyes.
2-Enlil punished the Sons of God, and killed many. However, a great number escaped to distant lands and to other continents.

65,000 B.C.:
This era marks the dawn of the modern human race, when and where the final form/format and characteristics of the human body took shape.

In other words, and simply put, today's humans are a carbon copy of their ancestors who lived 65,000 years ago. Grosso modo, this is the beginning of the existence of the human race as we know it today.

Because of its primordial genetic and historic importance, this date inspired an endless number of theorists, spiritual visionaries, channelers, mediums and ufologists to advance (Perhaps to fantasize as well) all sorts of scenarios and theories. Almost 99% of them were not aware of the genetic relation between Anunnaki and early inhabitants of Phoenicia.

A note on **Adamu:** One of the earliest forms of humans.

Adamu was the result of a genetic manipulation by the Anunnaki, who captured quasi-humans who lived on Earth, and upgraded their genes. This primordial quasi-human race is totally unrelated to modern humans.

From Adamu, the Biblical name Adam was derived.

The ancient Anunnaki/Sumerian texts referred to the Adamu race (Adamah) as primitive creatures. Worth mentioning here, that several quasi-human races already existed on Earth, long before the Anunnaki, the Igigi and the Lyrans landed on Earth.

A passage from the book "Ilmu Al Donia" described these "archaic races" as animals resembling humans.

Some had three legs, others crawled, while many other species had deformed bodies and totally lacked the mental faculties of modern Man.

In another passage of the book, Adamu were also called Adamah, and Baha'ema. From Baha'ema, the Arabic word Bahaaem is derived, which means animals.

The proto-Hebrew word Behemoth means the very same thing.

A note on **Akamu "Akama"**: Anunnaki/Ulemite/Assyrian. Noun. In Assyrian, Akamu means gathering; assembly; group of people. It is derived from the Ana'kh Akama. From Akamu, the Arabic word Kawmu is derived, which means exactly the same thing.

According to Ulema Fadel Al Bakri Al Qaysi, the Akama were created by the Anunnaki to administer and control the Akama-ra in quarantined areas in the Middle East. They established the rules of mating with the Anunnaki's "Women of Light", also known as "B'nat Nour".

During their first interaction with Earth's quasi-humans, and later on with humans, the Anunnaki feared that the Akamu could or would mate or date with another category of beings they have created from non-terrestrial genes.

Some of these extraterrestrial beings were created on Ashtari, and others in the Arab Peninsula. Among them were the "Women of Light" as they were called by the inhabitants of the area. The Akama were assigned the duty of supervising the Women of Light and the Akama-ra.

A note on Akama-ra: The Ulema said that the Akama-ra were the first beings who were allowed by Enki and Inanna to date the "Women of Light", who were quarantined on Earth by the Anunnaki.

The Akama-ra were genetically created by the Anunnaki on Ashtari, and were transported to planet Earth on Anunnaki spaceships, which are called Merkabah.

A note on Bashar: According to the Ulema, the Bashar (Human beings) appeared on planet Earth in a multitude of forms and shapes.

Excerpt from their Kira'at (Reading):

On planet Earth, there existed many different human races for millions of years. Some are known to us, while many others are totally unknown, because they have vanished without leaving a trace. The truth is that they have left many traces, but we have not discovered them yet. In the near future, we will discover some of their remains, and a new chapter on the history of mankind will be written.

However in 2003, skeletons of four vanished early forms of humans who did not look like humans, were discovered by English archeologists and anthropologists, but were shrouded in secrecy, and their discoveries were never made public for many reasons.

Two leading and extremely powerful Catholic theologians were behind the cover-up. Some of those early quasi-human forms were 10 feet tall, and others less than 3 feet tall, and looked like hobbits. Those species were created by various extraterrestrial races. The Anunnaki did not take part in the creation process of these very tall and very small quasi-humans.

The extraterrestrials created them here on planet Earth. But there are other early human beings who were created in space, and on other planets, and like the very small and very tall species, they were not part of the evolutionary process of the modern human beings.

In total, 36 (some say 46) different human and quasi-human species lived on planet Earth in many regions of the globe. And none of them were created by the "God" we know and worship.

After all, they did not look like humans, and if we have to believe that humans were created in the image of "God", as Judaism, Christianity and Islam tell us, then, most certainly those early 36 different species who looked like ferocious beasts, were not made in the image of "God".

Because they were created in many regions of planet Earth, and interbred around the globe, new horrifying species populated the Earth.

A note on Anafar Jin Markah: Nafar Jinmarkah, is the name of humans who walked on three legs. They were created by the Igigi, and later on were upgraded by the Anunnaki. The Igigi actually experimented quite a bit with the early human-forms.

First, they created the "Nafar Jinmarkah" meaning 'individual on three legs.'

They consisted of a very strong physical body but lacked agility. These bodies were created to carry heavy weight. Later on, the Igigi worked on a new human form that consisted of a body with two legs, in order to bring speed and better agility.

Yet, early humans remained terrifying, nothing like the Biblical descriptions.

49,000-45,000 B.C.:
Ninhursag and Enki appointed humans of an of Anunnaki origin to rule Shuruppak. More Anunnaki visits to Phoenicia.
The Island of Arwad becomes a very active Anunnaki center.

49,000 B.C.:
Massive migrations of humans to Europe, resulting in the early confrontations with the Neanderthals, but managed to cohabit and intermix with them.

13,000 B.C.:
Enlil hides his plans for the human race.
He confers with geneticists to decide on the fate of humans.

12,000-10,500 B.C.:
1-The Ice Age comes to an end. Chinese astrologers witnessed an exceptional movement in the skies accompanied by the descent of a celestial race from Sirius. They called this extraterrestrial race the "Dropa".
2-Enki instructs Ziusudra-Noah to build a submersible ship. The Deluge sweeps over planet Earth.

7,000 B.C.:
New Anunnaki's colonies are established in Tyre, Afka, Amchit and Baalbeck.

4,750 B.C.:
The first Assyrian temple is erected housing the secret language of the Anunnaki. This year marked the first trip of humans to Nibiru and neighboring stars. Upon their return to Earth, the Sumerian astronomers began to map the universe, and write the illustrative history of their gods and kings.
According to New Thought writers, this included an elaborate epic of the Anunnaki depicting them as gods who came to Earth from Sirius, Mars and the Pleiades. The Ulema disagree.

4,000 B.C.:
The word Kassi was a title first used by the Phoenicians and later was adopted by the Babylonians who ruled the Mesopotamian empire. Kassi also appeared as a Phoenician name in Egypt and Cassi was an inspiration for the ruling kings known as Catti in pre-Roman Britain. One minted 'Cas' coins featured the sun-horse and other Phoenician solar symbols.

3,800 B.C.: The Anunnaki began to urbanize their cities in Eridu and Nippur. The city of Erech is built in honor of Anu. Anu was the lord of the heavens, the heaven supreme god, and the chief god of the Annunaki.

A Babylonian slab almanac, mentioning the positions of the planets.

Babylonian tablet mentioning the comet of Halley.

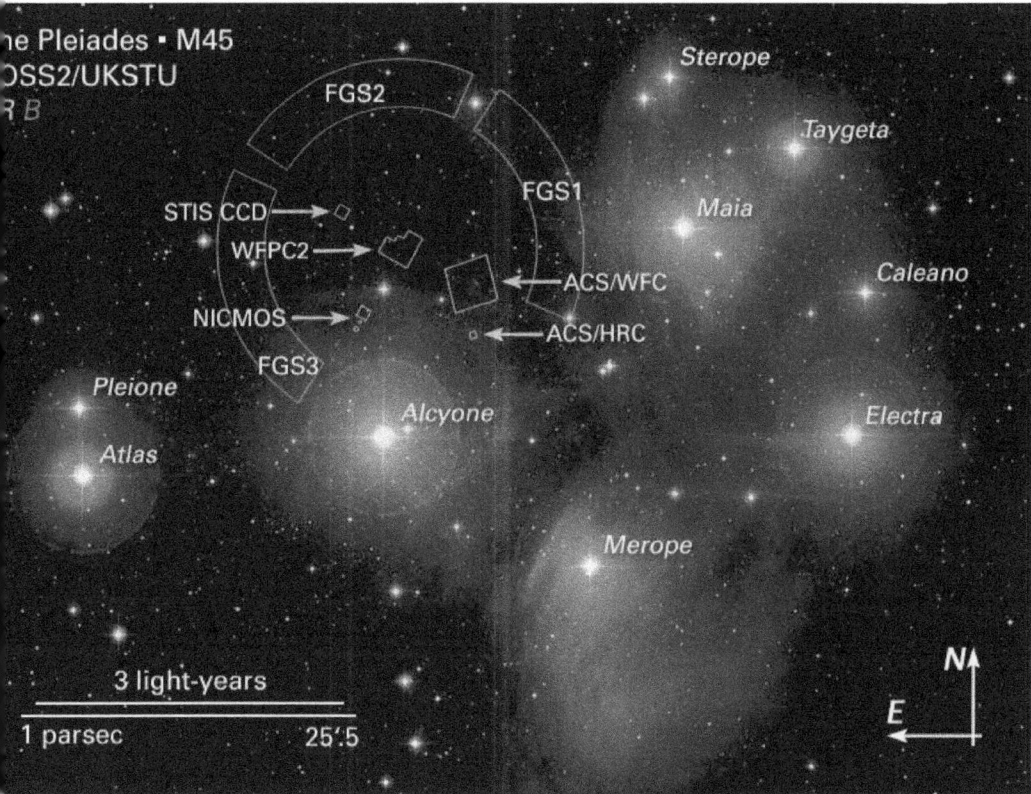

The Pleiades, also called as M45 is the brightest constellation in the night sky. It is close to the Orion Constellation.
The Anunnaki did NOT come from the Pleiades!

Anu is known to the Egyptians as Anu, to the Mesopotamian and Babylonians as An, and to the Akkadians as Anum. Anu is Niudimmud's father, and the son of Kishar and Anshar. Antu was his wife.

Their union created many children known as the Anunnaki. His sons were Enlil, Ea, and Ninhursag, also called Ninkhursag.

3,760 B.C.: Kish becomes a great capital. The calendar began at Nippur.

3,550 B.C.: The early Phoenician white Aryan race from the Caucasus Mountains region moved into the Indus Valley of India, and created what is today known as the Hindu religion.
They erected a shrine for the Anunnaki goddess Inanna.

Dingirs and vizirs paying homage to god Enlil "Anu".

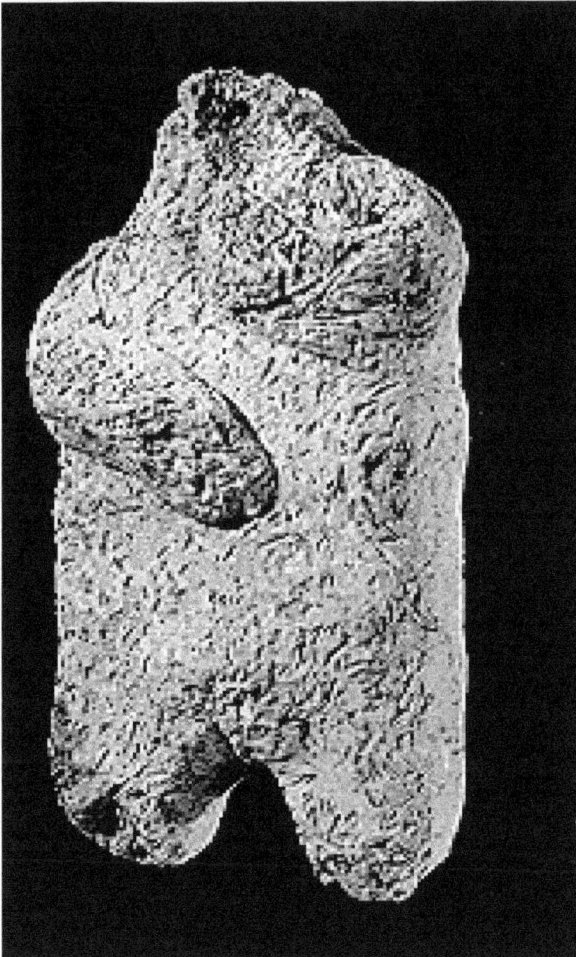

Figurine of a person in pain from Nippur.

Figurine of a person in pain from Nippur.

Akkadian seal showing Gilgamesh and Enkidu meeting the great
God Anu in the Apsu (The Square).

Inanna's escort and guardian.
Inanna's guardian, circa 3200-3000 B.C. Late Uruk. Jemdet Nasr
period. Cylinder seal. Mesopotamia.

The seal depicts a bearded man that has appeared on several
Mesopotamian-Babylonian artifacts excavated at Uruk, Inanna's
city. The man served Inanna as her consort and guardian, and
accompanied her to her wedding ceremony. Notice the curving
branches ending in rosette-flowers. The rosettes are the symbol of
Inanna. Because of the ritual aspect of the scene, we can conclude
that this event happened inside her temple.
Some Assysriologists have stated that this scene shows Dumuzi
being captured in the Sumerian Garden of Eden, called Edin in
Akkadian/Sumerian, and bound by the Ugalla demons who carry
him off to Kurnugi (The Babylonian underworld.)
In Mesopotamian and Babylonian mythologies, Dumuzi is the
consort of Inanna who has been identified and/or associated with
the Phoenician goddess Ishtar (Ashtaroot), the lover of Adon in
the Phoenician mythology.

3,450 B.C.:
Babylon became the principal spaceship terminal on earth. New launching pads were created.
Marduck revisited the early Anunnaki cities in Phoenicia. Mutiny against Marduck led to his arrest and imprisonment. He was exiled to Egypt, and later locked up inside the Great Pyramid. Followers of the new ruler threw the kingdom in state of chaos and complete disorder.

This brick of Ur-Cur, King of Ur, tells us about the building of a temple dedicated to goddess Ninni, located in the city of Erech.

215

A group of architects from Phoenicia, Babylon and Hadramoot built the Tower of Babel. To accomplish this project, they needed a large manpower.

Thus, they began to enslave the population and many inhabitants from neighboring countries. Chaos and confusion reigned over the cities of Sumer.

Many lost their mental faculties and became totally disoriented, and became unable to communicate with each other. This led to mass confusion which resulted in the destruction of the Tower of Babel.

Hadramout, Yemen.

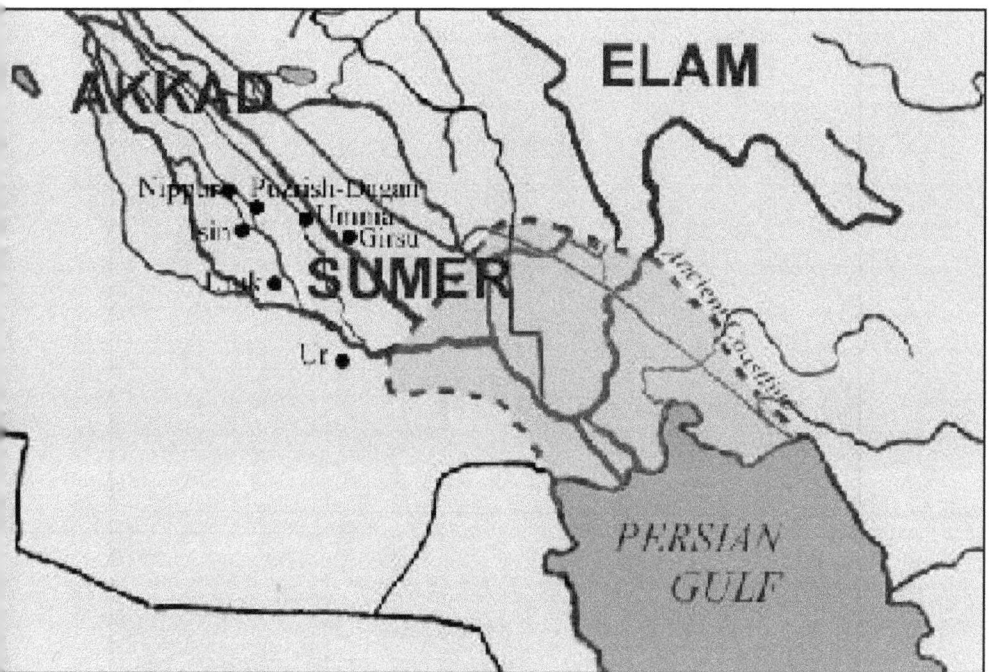

Map showing the location of Sumer, Akkad and Elam.

The Tower of Babel as envisaged in the medieval ages.

Babel is composed of two words:

a-Bab, which means a door. Alternative names are Al-Bab, Babu, Babi, in Arabic, Assyrian, Sumerian, Akkadia, respectively.

b-El, which means god, and/or master. Alternative names are EL (Ehl), Allah, Eli, Il, in Phoenician/Ugaritic, Arabic, Aramaic, Hebrew, and proto-Babylonian.

Thus, the word Babel means the gate and/or door of God, the Babylonian/Mesopotamian god, that is.

3,100 B.C.:
This year marks the restoration of law and order in Egypt, and the end of 350 tumultuous years of anarchy. Narmer, (also called Menes), the first Egyptian Pharaoh ascends to the throne in the city of Memphis. Narmer came from the north and conquered the south. His conquest united Egypt. Narmer founded Memphis as the first capital of united Egypt. The city of Thebes became the next capital of Egypt. During the reign of King Akhenaten, Amarna became the capital of the kingdom of Egypt.

Ruins of Amarna.

219

Published by

Times Square Press
New York, Berlin
Website: www.timessquarepress.com

Printed in the
United States of America and Germany
2014

www.ingramcontent.com/pod-product-compliance
Lightning Source LLC
Chambersburg PA
CBHW020610270326
41927CB00005B/257